JOHN
MacARTHUR

LUKE

The Savior of the World

THOMAS NELSON

Since 1798

NASHVILLE DALLAS MEXICO CITY RIO DE JANEIRO BEIJING

LUKE
MACARTHUR BIBLE STUDIES

Published by Nelson Impact, a Division of Thomas Nelson, Inc., P.O. Box 141000, Nashville, Tennessee 37214.

Produced with the assistance of the Livingstone Corporation. Project staff include Jake Barton, Mary Horner Collins, and Andy Culbertson.

Project editor: Len Woods

Scripture quotations marked NKJV are taken from *The Holy Bible*, New King James Version®. Copyright © 1979, 1980, 1982, 1992 Thomas Nelson, Inc. Publishers.

"Keys to the Text" and "Truth for Today" material is taken from the following sources:

1 Corinthians (electronic ed.). Copyright © 1984, 1996 by John MacArthur. MacArthur New Testament Commentary Series. Published by Moody Press, Chicago, Illinois. Used by permission.

God in the Manger. Copyright © 2001 by John MacArthur. W Publishing Group, a division of Thomas Nelson, Inc.

The MacArthur Quick Reference Guide to the Bible. Copyright © 2001 by John MacArthur. W Publishing Group, a division of Thomas Nelson, Inc.

The MacArthur Study Bible (electronic ed.). John MacArthur, General Editor. Copyright © 1997 by Word Publishing, a division of Thomas Nelson, Inc. All rights reserved. Used by permission.

Matthew, 1–7, 8–15, 16–23, 24–28 (electronic ed.). MacArthur New Testament Commentary Series. Copyright © 1989 by John MacArthur. Published by Moody Press, Chicago, Illinois. Used by permission.

Truth for Today: A Daily Touch of God's Grace. Copyright © 2001 by John MacArthur. Published by J. Countryman Publishers, Nashville, Tennessee.

Twelve Ordinary Men. Copyright © 2002 by John MacArthur. W Publishing Group, a division of Thomas Nelson, Inc.

Cover Art by Kirk Luttrell, Livingstone Corporation

Interior Design and Composition by Joel Bartlett, Livingstone Corporation

ISBN-10: 1-4185-0961-2
ISBN-13: 978-1-4185-0961-3

Printed in the United States of America.
08 09 RRD 9 8 7 6 5 4 3 2

CONTENTS

Introduction to Luke

As with the other three Gospels, the title is derived from the author's name. According to tradition, Luke was a Gentile. The apostle Paul seems to confirm this, distinguishing Luke from those who were "of the circumcision" (Col. 4:11, 14). That would make Luke the only Gentile to pen any books of Scripture. He is responsible for a significant portion of the New Testament, having written both this Gospel and the book of Acts.

Very little is known about Luke. He almost never included personal details about himself, and nothing definite is known about his background or his conversion. Both Eusebius and Jerome identified him as a native of Antioch (which may explain why so much of the book of Acts centers on Antioch—see Acts 11:19–27; 13:1–3; 14:26; 15:22–23, 30–35; 18:22–23). Luke was a frequent companion of the apostle Paul, at least from the time of Paul's Macedonian vision (Acts 16:9, 10) right up to the time of Paul's martyrdom (2 Tim. 4:11).

The apostle Paul referred to Luke as a physician (Col. 4:14). Luke's interest in medical phenomena is evident in the high profile he gave to Jesus' healing ministry (e.g., 4:38–40; 5:15–25; 6:17–19; 7:11–15; 8:43–47, 49–56; 9:2, 6, 11; 13:11–13; 14:2–4; 17:12–14; 22:50–51). In Luke's day, physicians did not have a unique vocabulary of technical terminology; so when Luke discusses healings and other medical issues, his language is not markedly different from that of the other Gospel writers.

Author and Date

The gospel of Luke and the book of Acts clearly were written by the same individual (see 1:1–4; Acts 1:1). Although he never identified himself by name, it is clear from his use of "we" in many sections of Acts that he was a close companion of the apostle Paul (Acts 16:10–17; 20:5–15; 21:1–18; 27:1–28:16). Luke is the only person, among the colleagues Paul mentions in his own epistles (Col. 4:14; 2 Tim. 4:11; Philem. 24), who fits the profile of the author of these books. That accords perfectly with the earliest tradition of the church, which unanimously attributed this Gospel to Luke.

Luke and Acts appear to have been written at about the same time—Luke first, then Acts. Combined, they make a two-volume work addressed to "Theophilus" (1:3; Acts 1:1), giving a sweeping history of the founding of Christianity, from the birth of Christ to Paul's imprisonment under house arrest in Rome (Acts 28:30–31).

The book of Acts ends with Paul still in Rome, which leads to the conclusion that Luke wrote these books from Rome during Paul's imprisonment there (ca. AD 60–62). Luke records Jesus' prophecy of the destruction of Jerusalem in AD 70 (19:42–44; 21:20–24) but makes no mention of the fulfillment of that prophecy, either here or in Acts. Luke made it a point to record such prophetic fulfillments (see Acts 11:28), so it is extremely unlikely he wrote these books after the Roman invasion of Jerusalem. Acts also includes no mention of the great persecution that began under Nero in AD 64. In addition, many scholars set the date of James's martyrdom at AD 62, and if that was before Luke completed his history, he certainly would have mentioned it. So, the most likely date for this Gospel is AD 60 or 61.

Background and Setting

Luke dedicated his works to "most excellent Theophilus" (literally "lover of God"—1:3; see Acts 1:1). This designation, which may be a nickname or a pseudonym, is accompanied by a formal address ("most excellent")—possibly signifying that "Theophilus" was a well-known Roman dignitary, perhaps one of those who had turned to Christ in "Caesar's household" (Phil. 4:22).

It is almost certain, however, that Luke envisioned a much broader audience for his work than this one man. The dedications at the outset of Luke and Acts are like the formal dedication in a modern book. They are not like the address of an epistle.

Luke expressly stated that his knowledge of the events recorded in his Gospel came from the reports of those who were eyewitnesses (1:1–2)—strongly implying that he himself was not an eyewitness. It is clear from his prologue that his aim was to give an ordered account of the events of Jesus' life, but this does not mean he followed a strict chronological order in all instances.

By acknowledging that he had compiled his account from various extant sources, Luke was not disclaiming divine inspiration for his work. The process of inspiration never bypasses or overrides the personalities, vocabularies, and styles of the human authors of Scripture. The unique traits of the human authors are always indelibly stamped on all the books of Scripture. Luke's research is no exception to this rule. The research itself was orchestrated by divine Providence. And in his writing, Luke was moved by the Spirit of God (2 Pet. 1:21). Therefore, his account is infallibly true.

Historical and Theological Themes

Luke's style is that of a scholarly, well-read author. He wrote as a meticulous historian, often giving details that helped identify the historical context of the events he described (1:5; 2:1–2; 3:1–2; 13:1–4).

A running theme in Luke's gospel is Jesus' compassion for Gentiles, Samaritans, women, children, tax collectors, sinners, and others often regarded as outcasts in Israel. Every time the Gospel mentions a tax collector, it is in a positive sense (3:12; 5:27; 7:29; 15:1; 18:10–13; 19:2). Yet, Luke did not ignore the salvation of those who were rich and respectable—e.g., 23:50–53. From the outset of Jesus' public ministry (4:18) to the Lord's final words on the cross (23:40–43), Luke underscored this theme of Christ's ministry to the pariahs of society. Again and again he showed how the Great Physician ministered to those most aware of their need (see 5:31–32; 15:4–7; 31–32; 19:10).

The high profile Luke accords to women is particularly significant. From the nativity account, where Mary, Elizabeth, and Anna are given prominence (chs. 1–2), to the events of resurrection morning, in which women again are major characters (24:1, 10), Luke emphasized the central role of women in the life and ministry of our Lord (7:12–15, 37–50; 8:2–3, 43–48; 10:38–42; 13:11–13; 21:2–4; 23:27–29, 49, 55–56).

Several other recurring themes form threads through Luke's gospel. Examples of these are human fear in the presence of God; forgiveness (3:3; 5:20–25; 6:37; 7:41–50; 11:4; 12:10; 17:3–4; 23:34; 24:47); joy; wonder at the mysteries of divine truth; the role of the Holy Spirit (1:15, 35, 41, 67; 2:25–27; 3:16, 22; 4:1, 14, 18; 10:21; 11:13; 12:10, 12); the temple in Jerusalem (1:9–22; 2:27–38, 46–49; 4:9–13; 18:10–14; 19:45–48; 20:1–21:6; 21:37–38; 24:53); and Jesus' prayers.

Starting with 9:51, Luke devotes ten chapters of his narrative to a travelogue of Jesus' final journey to Jerusalem. Much of the material in this section is unique to Luke. This is the heart of Luke's gospel, and it features a theme Luke stressed throughout: Jesus' relentless progression toward the cross. This was the very purpose for which Christ had come to earth (see 9:22–23; 17:25; 18:31–33; 24:25–26, 46), and He would not be deterred. The saving of sinners was His whole mission (19:10).

INTERPRETIVE CHALLENGES

Luke, like Mark, and in contrast to Matthew, appears to target a Gentile readership. He identified locations that would have been familiar to all Jews (4:31; 23:51; 24:13), suggesting that his audience went beyond those who already had knowledge of Palestinian geography. He usually preferred Greek terminology over Hebraisms (e.g., "Calvary" instead of "Golgotha" in 23:33). The other Gospels all use occasional Semitic terms such as "Abba" (Mark 14:36), "rabbi" (Matt. 23:7, 8; John 1:38, 49), and "hosanna" (Matt. 21:9; Mark 11:9, 10; John 12:13)—but Luke either omits them or uses Greek equivalents.

Luke quoted the Old Testament more sparingly than Matthew, and when citing Old Testament passages, he nearly always employed the Septuagint, a Greek translation of the Hebrew Scriptures. Furthermore, most of Luke's Old Testament citations are allusions rather than direct quotations, and many of them appear in Jesus' words rather than Luke's narration (2:23–4; 3:4–6; 4:4, 8, 10–12, 18–19; 7:27; 10:27; 18:20; 19:46; 20:17–18, 37, 42–43; 22:37).

Luke, more than any of the other Gospel writers, highlighted the universal scope of the gospel invitation. He portrayed Jesus as the Son of Man, rejected by Israel, and then offered to the world. As noted previously (see Historical and Theological Themes, page 2), Luke repeatedly related accounts of Gentiles, Samaritans, and other outcasts who found grace in Jesus' eyes. This emphasis is precisely what we would expect from a close companion of the "apostle to the Gentiles" (Rom. 11:13 NKJV).

Yet some critics have claimed to see a wide gap between Luke's theology and that of Paul. It is true that Luke's gospel is practically devoid of terminology that is uniquely Pauline. Luke wrote with his own style. Yet the underlying theology is perfectly in harmony with that of the apostle's. The centerpiece of Paul's doctrine is justification by faith. Luke also highlighted and illustrated justification by faith in many of the incidents and parables he related, chiefly the account of the Pharisee and the publican (18:9–14); the familiar story of the prodigal son (15:11–32); the incident at Simon's house (7:36–50); and the salvation of Zacchaeus (19:1–10).

~ I ~
CHRIST'S BIRTH AND BOYHOOD

DRAWING NEAR

Babies are born every day, but Jesus' birth was unique. What is one special way you and your family celebrate Jesus' birth?

_____

_____

_____

_____

_____

Jesus was twelve when he visited the temple. Think back to when you were twelve years old. What were you like? What were your interests? Were you involved in church or interested in spiritual things?

_____

_____

_____

_____

_____

THE CONTEXT

Though attended by great heavenly fanfare, Jesus' birth generated little notice or interest among men. Only a few obscure witnesses celebrated the blessed arrival of the Savior into our sin-scarred world. Luke alone reports the unusual circumstances surrounding the birth of John the Baptist, the annunciation to Mary, the manger, the angelic visitation to the shepherds, and the Spirit-led responses of Simeon and Anna when Jesus was presented at the temple. Of the Gospel writers, only Luke provides any information about the childhood of Christ (2:40–52). But even these details are sketchy, confined mostly to the familiar story of Jesus' encounter with the teachers at the temple when He was twelve. As you read the opening of Luke's story, try to imagine what it must have been like when Jesus first came into the world.

5

KEYS TO THE TEXT

Luke's Purpose: Writing primarily to a man named Theophilus and for a Gentile audience, Luke set out to construct a careful and comprehensive account of the life of Christ. His goal was to show that Jesus is not only the long-awaited Messiah of the Jews, but also the Savior of non-Jews. A meticulous historian, Luke begins at the beginning. His account of the nativity is the fullest in all the Gospel records and more polished in its literary style.

Jesus: A name from the Greek word *Iesous,* equivalent to the Hebrew name *Yeshua* (Joshua), that literally means, "The LORD shall save." In Old Testament times, the name *Jesus* was a common Jewish name. However, the meaning of this name expresses Jesus' unique redemptive work on earth. The angel sent to Joseph affirmed the importance of Jesus' name, "for He will save His people from their sins" (Matt. 1:21 NKJV).

UNLEASHING THE TEXT

Read 1:1–2:52, noting the key words and definitions next to the passage.

many (v. 1)—Although Luke wrote direct, divine revelation inspired by the Holy Spirit, he also acknowledged the works of others. Further, he was personally acquainted with many firsthand witnesses to the events of Christ's life.

having had perfect understanding (v. 3)—Literally "having traced out carefully"; Luke's gospel was the result of painstaking investigation.

most excellent (v. 3)—This was a title used to address governors (Acts 23:26; 24:3; 26:25). This sort of language was reserved for the highest dignitaries, suggesting that Theophilus was a such a person.

certainty (v. 4)—Note the implicit claim of authority. Though Luke drew from other sources (v. 3), he regarded the reliability and authority of his Gospel as superior to uninspired sources.

both righteous before God (v. 6)—They were believers, justified in God's sight. There is a clear echo of Pauline theology in this expression.

Luke 1:1–2:52 (NKJV)

1 *Inasmuch as many have taken in hand to set in order a narrative of those things which have been fulfilled among us,*

2 *just as those who from the beginning were eyewitnesses and ministers of the word delivered them to us,*

3 *it seemed good to me also, having had perfect understanding of all things from the very first, to write to you an orderly account, most excellent Theophilus,*

4 *that you may know the certainty of those things in which you were instructed.*

5 *There was in the days of Herod, the king of Judea, a certain priest named Zacharias, of the division of Abijah. His wife was of the daughters of Aaron, and her name was Elizabeth.*

6 *And they were both righteous before God, walking in all the commandments and ordinances of the Lord blameless.*

7 *But they had no child, because Elizabeth was barren, and they were both well advanced in years.*

8 *So it was, that while he was serving as priest before God in the order of his division,*

9 *according to the custom of the priesthood, his lot fell to burn incense when he went into the temple of the Lord.*

10 *And the whole multitude of the people was praying outside at the hour of incense.*

11 *Then an angel of the Lord appeared to him, standing on the right side of the altar of incense.*

12 *And when Zacharias saw him, he was troubled, and fear fell upon him.*

13 *But the angel said to him, "Do not be afraid, Zacharias, for your prayer is heard; and your wife Elizabeth will bear you a son, and you shall call his name John.*

14 *And you will have joy and gladness, and many will rejoice at his birth.*

15 *For he will be great in the sight of the Lord, and shall drink neither wine nor strong drink. He will also be filled with the Holy Spirit, even from his mother's womb.*

16 *And he will turn many of the children of Israel to the Lord their God.*

17 *He will also go before Him in the spirit and power of Elijah, 'to turn the hearts of the fathers to the children,' and the disobedient to the wisdom of the just, to make ready a people prepared for the Lord."*

18 *And Zacharias said to the angel, "How shall I know this? For I am an old man, and my wife is well advanced in years."*

19 *And the angel answered and said to him, "I am Gabriel, who stands in the presence of God, and was sent to speak to you and bring you these glad tidings.*

20 *But behold, you will be mute and not able to speak until the day these things take place, because you did not believe my words which will be fulfilled in their own time."*

his lot fell to burn incense (v. 9)—Because of the large number of priests, most would never be chosen for such a duty; Zacharias no doubt regarded this as the supreme moment in a lifetime of priestly service.

fear (v. 12)—the normal response—and an appropriate one—when someone is confronted by a divine visitation or a mighty work of God

joy and gladness (v. 14)—Both are hallmarks of the messianic kingdom.

in the spirit and power of Elijah (v. 17)—Elijah was known for his bold, uncompromising stand for the Word of God—even in the face of a ruthless monarch.

Gabriel (v. 19)—literally "strong man of God"; one of only two holy angels whose names are given in Scripture (the other is Michael)

my reproach (v. 25)—Childlessness carried a social stigma in a culture where blessings were tied to birthrights and family lines; barrenness could occasionally be a sign of divine disfavor.

a virgin (v. 27)—A right view of Christ's incarnation (i.e. His deity and sinlessness) hinges on the truth that Jesus was virgin born.

highly favored (v. 28)—Literally "full of grace"—this term is used of all believers in Ephesians 1:6, where it is translated "accepted." Mary was a recipient, not a dispenser, of divine grace.

the Son of the Highest (v. 32)—The angel was telling Mary that her Son would be equal to the Most High God.

I do not know a man (v. 34)—I.e., conjugally. Mary understood that the angel was speaking of an immediate conception, and she and Joseph were still in the midst of the long engagement period.

21 *And the people waited for Zacharias, and marveled that he lingered so long in the temple.*

22 *But when he came out, he could not speak to them; and they perceived that he had seen a vision in the temple, for he beckoned to them and remained speechless.*

23 *So it was, as soon as the days of his service were completed, that he departed to his own house.*

24 *Now after those days his wife Elizabeth conceived; and she hid herself five months, saying,*

25 *"Thus the Lord has dealt with me, in the days when He looked on me, to take away my reproach among people."*

26 *Now in the sixth month the angel Gabriel was sent by God to a city of Galilee named Nazareth,*

27 *to a virgin betrothed to a man whose name was Joseph, of the house of David. The virgin's name was Mary.*

28 *And having come in, the angel said to her, "Rejoice, highly favored one, the Lord is with you; blessed are you among women!"*

29 *But when she saw him, she was troubled at his saying, and considered what manner of greeting this was.*

30 *Then the angel said to her, "Do not be afraid, Mary, for you have found favor with God.*

31 *And behold, you will conceive in your womb and bring forth a Son, and shall call His name Jesus.*

32 *He will be great, and will be called the Son of the Highest; and the Lord God will give Him the throne of His father David.*

33 *And He will reign over the house of Jacob forever, and of His kingdom there will be no end."*

34 *Then Mary said to the angel, "How can this be, since I do not know a man?"*

35 *And the angel answered and said to her, "The Holy Spirit will come upon you, and the power of the Highest will overshadow you; therefore, also, that Holy One who is to be born will be called the Son of God.*

36 *Now indeed, Elizabeth your relative has also conceived a son in her old age; and this is now the sixth month for her who was called barren.*

37 *For with God nothing will be impossible."*

38 *Then Mary said, "Behold the maidservant of the Lord! Let it be to me according to your word." And the angel departed from her.*

39 *Now Mary arose in those days and went into the hill country with haste, to a city of Judah,*

40 *and entered the house of Zacharias and greeted Elizabeth.*

41 *And it happened, when Elizabeth heard the greeting of Mary, that the babe leaped in her womb; and Elizabeth was filled with the Holy Spirit.*

42 *Then she spoke out with a loud voice and said, "Blessed are you among women, and blessed is the fruit of your womb!*

43 *But why is this granted to me, that the mother of my Lord should come to me?*

44 *For indeed, as soon as the voice of your greeting sounded in my ears, the babe leaped in my womb for joy.*

the babe leaped in my womb for joy (v. 44)—The infant, like his mother, was Spirit-filled.

45 *Blessed is she who believed, for there will be a fulfillment of those things which were told her from the Lord."*

46 *And Mary said: "My soul magnifies the Lord,*

47 *And my spirit has rejoiced in God my Savior.*

48 *For He has regarded the lowly state of His maidservant; for behold, henceforth all generations will call me blessed.*

49 *For He who is mighty has done great things for me, and holy is His name.*

50 *And His mercy is on those who fear Him from generation to generation.*

51 *He has shown strength with His arm; He has scattered the proud in the imagination of their hearts.*

52 *He has put down the mighty from their thrones, and exalted the lowly.*

53 *He has filled the hungry with good things, and the rich He has sent away empty.*

54 *He has helped His servant Israel, in remembrance of His mercy,*

55 *As He spoke to our fathers, to Abraham and to his seed forever."*

56 *And Mary remained with her about three months, and returned to her house.*

57 *Now Elizabeth's full time came for her to be delivered, and she brought forth a son.*

58 *When her neighbors and relatives heard how the Lord had shown great mercy to her, they rejoiced with her.*

59 *So it was, on the eighth day, that they came to circumcise the child; and they would have called him by the name of his father, Zacharias.*

60 *His mother answered and said, "No; he shall be called John."*

61 *But they said to her, "There is no one among your relatives who is called by this name."*

62 *So they made signs to his father—what he would have him called.*

63 *And he asked for a writing tablet, and wrote, saying, "His name is John." So they all marveled.*

64 *Immediately his mouth was opened and his tongue loosed, and he spoke, praising God.*

65 *Then fear came on all who dwelt around them; and all these sayings were discussed throughout all the hill country of Judea.*

66 *And all those who heard them kept them in their hearts, saying, "What kind of child will this be?" And the hand of the Lord was with him.*

67 *Now his father Zacharias was filled with the Holy Spirit, and prophesied, saying:*

68 *"Blessed is the Lord God of Israel, For He has visited and redeemed His people,*

69 *And has raised up a horn of salvation for us in the house of His servant David,*

70 *As He spoke by the mouth of His holy prophets, who have been since the world began,*

the eighth day (v. 59)—In accord with God's commandment (Lev. 12:1–3), it had become customary to name a child at circumcision.

horn of salvation (v. 69)—a common Old Testament expression symbolizing strength

71 *That we should be saved from our enemies and from the hand of all who hate us,*

72 *To perform the mercy promised to our fathers and to remember His holy covenant,*

73 *The oath which He swore to our father Abraham:*

74 *To grant us that we, being delivered from the hand of our enemies, might serve Him without fear,*

75 *In holiness and righteousness before Him all the days of our life.*

76 *"And you, child, will be called the prophet of the Highest; for you will go before the face of the Lord to prepare His ways,*

77 *To give knowledge of salvation to His people by the remission of their sins,*

78 *Through the tender mercy of our God, with which the Dayspring from on high has visited us;*

Dayspring (v. 78)—a messianic reference (see Isa. 9:2; 60:1–3; Mal. 4:2; 2 Pet. 1:19; Rev. 22:16)

79 *To give light to those who sit in darkness and the shadow of death, to guide our feet into the way of peace."*

80 *So the child grew and became strong in spirit, and was in the deserts till the day of his manifestation to Israel.*

2:1 *And it came to pass in those days that a decree went out from Caesar Augustus that all the world should be registered.*

2 *This census first took place while Quirinius was governing Syria.*

3 *So all went to be registered, everyone to his own city.*

4 *Joseph also went up from Galilee, out of the city of Nazareth, into Judea, to the city of David, which is called Bethlehem, because he was of the house and lineage of David,*

Nazareth . . . Bethlehem (2:4)—Both Joseph and Mary (who was on the verge of delivery) were descendants of David and therefore went to their tribal home in Judea to be registered—a difficult trek of more than seventy miles through mountainous terrain.

5 *to be registered with Mary, his betrothed wife, who was with child.*

6 *So it was, that while they were there, the days were completed for her to be delivered.*

7 *And she brought forth her firstborn Son, and wrapped Him in swaddling cloths, and laid Him in a manger, because there was no room for them in the inn.*

firstborn (v. 7)—Mary had other children subsequent to this.

manger (v. 7)—a feeding trough for animals

a Savior (v. 11)—This verse and John 4:42 are the only two places in the Gospels where Christ is referred to as "Savior."

Lord (v. 11)—The Greek word can mean "master"—but here (and in most of its New Testament occurrences), it is used as a title of deity.

host (v. 13)—a term used to describe an army encampment or heavenly army

8 Now there were in the same country shepherds living out in the fields, keeping watch over their flock by night.

9 And behold, an angel of the Lord stood before them, and the glory of the Lord shone around them, and they were greatly afraid.

10 Then the angel said to them, "Do not be afraid, for behold, I bring you good tidings of great joy which will be to all people.

11 For there is born to you this day in the city of David a Savior, who is Christ the Lord.

12 And this will be the sign to you: You will find a Babe wrapped in swaddling cloths, lying in a manger."

13 And suddenly there was with the angel a multitude of the heavenly host praising God and saying:

14 "Glory to God in the highest, And on earth peace, goodwill toward men!"

15 So it was, when the angels had gone away from them into heaven, that the shepherds said to one another, "Let us now go to Bethlehem and see this thing that has come to pass, which the Lord has made known to us."

16 And they came with haste and found Mary and Joseph, and the Babe lying in a manger.

17 Now when they had seen Him, they made widely known the saying which was told them concerning this Child.

18 And all those who heard it marveled at those things which were told them by the shepherds.

19 But Mary kept all these things and pondered them in her heart.

20 Then the shepherds returned, glorifying and praising God for all the things that they had heard and seen, as it was told them.

21 And when eight days were completed for the circumcision of the Child, His name was called JESUS, the name given by the angel before He was conceived in the womb.

22 Now when the days of her purification according to

the law of Moses were completed, they brought Him to Jerusalem to present Him to the Lord

23 (as it is written in the law of the Lord, "Every male who opens the womb shall be called holy to the LORD"),

24 and to offer a sacrifice according to what is said in the law of the Lord, "A pair of turtledoves or two young pigeons."

25 And behold, there was a man in Jerusalem whose name was Simeon, and this man was just and devout, waiting for the Consolation of Israel, and the Holy Spirit was upon him.

26 And it had been revealed to him by the Holy Spirit that he would not see death before he had seen the Lord's Christ.

27 So he came by the Spirit into the temple. And when the parents brought in the Child Jesus, to do for Him according to the custom of the law,

28 he took Him up in his arms and blessed God and said:

29 "Lord, now You are letting Your servant depart in peace, According to Your word;

30 For my eyes have seen Your salvation

31 Which You have prepared before the face of all peoples,

32 A light to bring revelation to the Gentiles, And the glory of Your people Israel."

33 And Joseph and His mother marveled at those things which were spoken of Him.

34 Then Simeon blessed them, and said to Mary His mother, "Behold, this Child is destined for the fall and rising of many in Israel, and for a sign which will be spoken against

35 (yes, a sword will pierce through your own soul also), that the thoughts of many hearts may be revealed."

36 Now there was one, Anna, a prophetess, the daughter of Phanuel, of the tribe of Asher. She was of a great age, and had lived with a husband seven years from her virginity;

the Consolation of Israel (v. 25)—a messianic title, evidently derived from verses like Isaiah 25:9; 40:1–2; 66:1–11

all peoples (v. 31)—i.e., all nations, tongues, and tribes (see Rev. 7:9)—both Israel and the Gentiles (v. 32)

fall and rising of many in Israel (v. 34)—To those who reject Him, He is a stone of stumbling (1 Pet. 2:8); those who receive Him are raised up (Eph. 2:6).

a prophetess (v. 36)—This refers to a woman who spoke God's Word; a teacher of the Old Testament, not a source of revelation.

37 *and this woman was a widow of about eighty-four years, who did not depart from the temple, but served God with fastings and prayers night and day.*

38 *And coming in that instant she gave thanks to the Lord, and spoke of Him to all those who looked for redemption in Jerusalem.*

39 *So when they had performed all things according to the law of the Lord, they returned to Galilee, to their own city, Nazareth.*

40 *And the Child grew and became strong in spirit, filled with wisdom; and the grace of God was upon Him.*

41 *His parents went to Jerusalem every year at the Feast of the Passover.*

when He was twelve years old (v. 42)—*Bar mitzvah* (when a Jewish boy became a "son of the commandment") was at age thirteen, so most Jewish boys celebrated their first feast at age twelve, in preparation for that rite of passage into adulthood.

42 *And when He was twelve years old, they went up to Jerusalem according to the custom of the feast.*

43 *When they had finished the days, as they returned, the Boy Jesus lingered behind in Jerusalem. And Joseph and His mother did not know it;*

44 *but supposing Him to have been in the company, they went a day's journey, and sought Him among their relatives and acquaintances.*

45 *So when they did not find Him, they returned to Jerusalem, seeking Him.*

listening to them and asking them questions (v. 46)—Jesus was utterly respectful, taking the role of the student. But even at that young age, His questions showed a wisdom that put the teachers to shame.

46 *Now so it was that after three days they found Him in the temple, sitting in the midst of the teachers, both listening to them and asking them questions.*

47 *And all who heard Him were astonished at His understanding and answers.*

48 *So when they saw Him, they were amazed; and His mother said to Him, "Son, why have You done this to us? Look, Your father and I have sought You anxiously."*

My Father's business (v. 49)— Jesus was not demonstrating insolence, but genuine amazement that they did not know where to look for Him. Even at so young an age, He had a clear consciousness of His identity and mission.

49 *And He said to them, "Why did you seek Me? Did you not know that I must be about My Father's business?"*

50 *But they did not understand the statement which He spoke to them.*

51 *Then He went down with them and came to*

14

Nazareth, and was subject to them, but His mother kept all these things in her heart.

52 *And Jesus increased in wisdom and stature, and in favor with God and men.*

And Jesus increased (v. 52)— Jesus did not cease being God or divest Himself of divine attributes in order to become man; in his humanity He was subject to the normal process of human growth, intellectually, physically, spiritually, and socially.

1) Luke goes into great detail about the birth of John the Baptist. Why?

_____

_____

_____

_____

_____

_____

_____

2) What does Luke 1 reveal about Zacharias, the father of John? How would you describe this man in your own words?

_____

_____

_____

_____

_____

_____

3) Upon receiving the news that she would be the "mother of Israel's Messiah," Mary broke forth into praise. Summarize the content of her inspired song.

_____

_____

_____

_____

_____

_____

4) Following the birth of John, Zacharias was filled with the Holy Spirit and he began to prophesy. What descriptions and specific details are revealed about the important role Zacharias's son would play in the coming of the kingdom of God?

_____

_____

_____

_____

_____

5) What unexpected events transpired when Joseph and Mary came to present Jesus to the Lord at the temple?

_____

_____

_____

_____

_____

6) What do we know of Christ's childhood? What does Luke reveal?

_____

_____

_____

_____

7) Luke records the angel Gabriel's announcement to Mary, and her submissive, faith-filled response, "Let it be to me according to your word" (v. 38 NKJV). What does this teach you about surrender to the sovereign will of God?

_____

_____

_____

_____

Going Deeper

Read Matthew 1:18–2:3, 9–11, the other primary Gospel account of the coming of Christ into the world.

1:18 *Now the birth of Jesus Christ was as follows: After His mother Mary was betrothed to Joseph, before they came together, she was found with child of the Holy Spirit.*

19 *Then Joseph her husband, being a just man, and not wanting to make her a public example, was minded to put her away secretly.*

20 *But while he thought about these things, behold, an angel of the Lord appeared to him in a dream, saying, "Joseph, son of David, do not be afraid to take to you Mary your wife, for that which is conceived in her is of the Holy Spirit.*

21 *And she will bring forth a Son, and you shall call His name JESUS, for He will save His people from their sins."*

22 *So all this was done that it might be fulfilled which was spoken by the Lord through the prophet, saying:*

23 *"Behold, the virgin shall be with child, and bear a Son, and they shall call His name Immanuel," which is translated, "God with us."*

24 *Then Joseph, being aroused from sleep, did as the angel of the Lord commanded him and took to him his wife,*

25 *and did not know her till she had brought forth her firstborn Son. And he called His name JESUS.*

2:1 *Now after Jesus was born in Bethlehem of Judea in the days of Herod the king, behold, wise men from the East came to Jerusalem,*

2 *saying, "Where is He who has been born King of the Jews? For we have seen His star in the East and have come to worship Him."*

3 *When Herod the king heard this, he was troubled, and all Jerusalem with him . . .*

9 *When they heard the king, they departed; and behold, the star which they had seen in the East went before them, till it came and stood over where the young Child was.*

10 *When they saw the star, they rejoiced with exceedingly great joy.*

11 *And when they had come into the house, they saw the young Child with Mary His mother, and fell down and worshiped Him. And when they had opened their treasures, they presented gifts to Him: gold, frankincense, and myrrh.*

Exploring the Meaning

8) What new facts and insights does Matthew's gospel give about Jesus' birth that are not found in Luke's gospel?

_____

_____

_____

_____

_____

9) Why is it significant that Mary referred to "God my Savior" in Luke v. 47 (NKJV)?

_____

_____

_____

_____

_____

10) Why do you think there are so many references to people wondering or marveling or breaking forth into praise in these chapters?

_____

_____

_____

_____

11) Some have suggested that the incident of Jesus being left (or remaining) at the temple reveals a boyish mischievousness on His part, or that His response to Mary was perhaps a bit disrespectful. How do you answer these charges?

_____

_____

_____

_____

TRUTH FOR TODAY

Many people doubt whether Jesus ever really existed, but many historians have written about Jesus Christ. Around AD 114, the Roman historian Tacitus wrote that "the founder of the Christian religion, Jesus Christ, was put to death by Pontius Pilate in the reign of the Roman Emperor Tiberius." Pliny the Younger wrote a letter to the Emperor Trajan on the subject of Christ and Christians. In AD 90, the Jewish historian Josephus penned a short biographical note on Jesus: "Now there was about this time Jesus, a wise man, if it be lawful to call Him a man, for He was a doer of wonderful works, a teacher of such men as received the truth with pleasure. He drew over to Him both many of the Jews and many of the Gentiles. He was Christ." The Talmud refers to Jesus of Nazareth. Jesus was a man in history. And His claims were true.

REFLECTING ON THE TEXT

12) Christ came into the world . . . of this there can be no doubt. The bigger question is, has He come into your heart? What do you think of Jesus?

---

13) Who are your favorite characters in these two opening chapters of Luke? What do you like about these individuals?

---

14) Luke 2:52 speaks of Jesus growing intellectually, physically, spiritually, and socially. What one thing can you do today in each of these areas to foster personal growth?

Personal Response

Write out additional reflections, questions you may have, or a prayer.

CHRIST'S MINISTRY BEGINS

DRAWING NEAR

As Jesus began His ministry, He encountered barriers and spiritual opposition. Think about a long-term project you've undertaken (e.g. a home renovation, a diet/exercise regimen, pursuing another degree, etc.)? What difficulties did you encounter?

_____

_____

_____

_____

What character qualities does it take to not only begin a task but also to see it through to the end?

_____

_____

_____

_____

THE CONTEXT

Luke heralds the beginning of Jesus' kingdom work by introducing John the Baptist, the forerunner of Christ. In those days, monarchs traveling in wilderness regions would have crews of workmen go ahead of them to make sure the road was clear of debris, obstructions, potholes, and other hazards that might make their journey difficult. In a spiritual sense, John paved the way for Christ, calling the people of Israel to prepare their hearts for the coming of their Messiah.

After Christ encounters real opposition in His forty-day temptation, we read of the inauguration of His ministry. Note how much of His ministry is to Gentiles (the widow of Zarephath and Naaman the Syrian). Both of these individuals lived during times of widespread unbelief in Israel. Jesus' point was that God bypassed all the widows and lepers in Israel, yet showed grace to two Gentiles. The theme of God's concern for Jews and Gentiles runs throughout Luke's gospel.

KEYS TO THE TEXT

Baptize: This word comes from the Greek *baptizo,* which means, "to dip" or "to immerse." People came to John the Baptist to be immersed by him in the Jordan River. The baptism of Gentile proselytes to Judaism was common to the Jews, but this kind of baptism for Jews was new and strange to them. John called them to be baptized as a public renunciation of their old way of life. Their baptism also symbolized the preparation of their hearts for the coming of the Messiah. Paul connected baptism with the believers' identification with Christ. Just as a cloth soaked in dye absorbs the color of the dye, so a person immersed in Christ should take on the nature of Christ.

Christ's Genealogy: Luke traces Christ's lineage in a genealogy that moves backward from Jesus to Adam. (Contrast this with the genealogy in Matthew's gospel, which moves forward, from Abraham to Joseph.) The two ancestral records are easily reconciled if Luke's is seen as Mary's genealogy, and Matthew's version represents Joseph's. Thus the royal line is passed through Jesus' legal father, and His physical descent from David is established by Mary's lineage.

UNLEASHING THE TEXT

Read 3:1–4:44, noting the key words and definitions next to the passage.

Luke 3:1–4:44 (NKJV)

1 Now in the fifteenth year of the reign of Tiberius Caesar, Pontius Pilate being governor of Judea, Herod being tetrarch of Galilee, his brother Philip tetrarch of Iturea and the region of Trachonitis, and Lysanias tetrarch of Abilene,

2 while Annas and Caiaphas were high priests, the word of God came to John the son of Zacharias in the wilderness.

for the remission of sins (v. 3)—i.e., to symbolize and testify of the forgiveness already received upon repentance

3 And he went into all the region around the Jordan, preaching a baptism of repentance for the remission of sins,

make His paths straight (v. 4)— quoted from Isaiah 40:3–5

4 as it is written in the book of the words of Isaiah the prophet, saying: "The voice of one crying in the wilderness: 'Prepare the way of the LORD; make His paths straight.

5 Every valley shall be filled and every mountain and

hill brought low; the crooked places shall be made straight and the rough ways smooth;

6 And all flesh shall see the salvation of God.' "

7 Then he said to the multitudes that came out to be baptized by him, "Brood of vipers! Who warned you to flee from the wrath to come?

8 Therefore bear fruits worthy of repentance, and do not begin to say to yourselves, 'We have Abraham as our father.' For I say to you that God is able to raise up children to Abraham from these stones.

9 And even now the ax is laid to the root of the trees. Therefore every tree which does not bear good fruit is cut down and thrown into the fire."

10 So the people asked him, saying, "What shall we do then?"

11 He answered and said to them, "He who has two tunics, let him give to him who has none; and he who has food, let him do likewise."

12 Then tax collectors also came to be baptized, and said to him, "Teacher, what shall we do?"

13 And he said to them, "Collect no more than what is appointed for you."

14 Likewise the soldiers asked him, saying, "And what shall we do?" So he said to them, "Do not intimidate anyone or accuse falsely, and be content with your wages."

15 Now as the people were in expectation, and all reasoned in their hearts about John, whether he was the Christ or not,

16 John answered, saying to all, "I indeed baptize you with water; but One mightier than I is coming, whose sandal strap I am not worthy to loose. He will baptize you with the Holy Spirit and fire.

17 His winnowing fan is in His hand, and He will thoroughly clean out His threshing floor, and gather the wheat into His barn; but the chaff He will burn with unquenchable fire."

18 And with many other exhortations he preached to the people.

all flesh (v. 6)—Gentiles as well as Jews. All four Gospels quote Isaiah 40:3 (Matt. 3:3; Mark 1:3; John 1:23). Only Luke adds vv. 5–6, thus using a familiar text from Isaiah to stress his theme of the universal scope of the Gospel.

children to Abraham (v. 8)—Abraham's true children are not merely physical descendants, but those who follow his faith, believing God's Word the way he did (Rom. 4:11–16; 9:8; Gal. 3:7).

two tunics (v. 11)—These were shirtlike garments. Because of the imminence of the coming judgment, this was not a time to hoard one's surplus goods.

soldiers (v. 14)—This refers to members of the occupying Roman army, hated by the Jewish people for their brutality and paganism. The fact that such people responded to John's preaching reveals the powerful influence his ministry had—especially on the outcasts of society.

sandal strap (v. 16)—Unfastening the sandal strap was the lowliest slave's task, preliminary to washing the feet.

shut John up in prison (v. 20)—
This event actually occurred much later during Jesus' ministry, but Luke organized his material on John the Baptist topically rather than chronologically.

while He prayed (v. 21)—
Prayer is one of Luke's dominant themes.

like a dove (v. 22)— picture of gentleness

about thirty years of age (v. 23)—a customary age for entering into the office of prophet (Ezek. 1:1), priest (Num. 4:3, 35, 39, 43, 47), or king (Gen. 41:46; 2 Sam. 5:4)

19 But Herod the tetrarch, being rebuked by him concerning Herodias, his brother Philip's wife, and for all the evils which Herod had done,

20 also added this, above all, that he shut John up in prison.

21 When all the people were baptized, it came to pass that Jesus also was baptized; and while He prayed, the heaven was opened.

22 And the Holy Spirit descended in bodily form like a dove upon Him, and a voice came from heaven which said, "You are My beloved Son; in You I am well pleased."

23 Now Jesus Himself began His ministry at about thirty years of age, being (as was supposed) the son of Joseph, the son of Heli,

24 the son of Matthat, the son of Levi, the son of Melchi, the son of Janna, the son of Joseph,

25 the son of Mattathiah, the son of Amos, the son of Nahum, the son of Esli, the son of Naggai,

26 the son of Maath, the son of Mattathiah, the son of Semei, the son of Joseph, the son of Judah,

27 the son of Joannas, the son of Rhesa, the son of Zerubbabel, the son of Shealtiel, the son of Neri,

28 the son of Melchi, the son of Addi, the son of Cosam, the son of Elmodam, the son of Er,

29 the son of Jose, the son of Eliezer, the son of Jorim, the son of Matthat, the son of Levi,

30 the son of Simeon, the son of Judah, the son of Joseph, the son of Jonan, the son of Eliakim,

31 the son of Melea, the son of Menan, the son of Mattathah, the son of Nathan, the son of David,

32 the son of Jesse, the son of Obed, the son of Boaz, the son of Salmon, the son of Nahshon,

33 the son of Amminadab, the son of Ram, the son of Hezron, the son of Perez, the son of Judah,

34 the son of Jacob, the son of Isaac, the son of Abraham, the son of Terah, the son of Nahor,

35 the son of Serug, the son of Reu, the son of Peleg, the son of Eber, the son of Shelah,

36 the son of Cainan, the son of Arphaxad, the son of
Shem, the son of Noah, the son of Lamech,

37 the son of Methuselah, the son of Enoch, the son of
Jared, the son of Mahalalel, the son of Cainan,

38 the son of Enosh, the son of Seth, the son of Adam,
the son of God.

4:1 Then Jesus, being filled with the Holy Spirit,
returned from the Jordan and was led by the Spirit
into the wilderness,

2 being tempted for forty days by the devil. And in
those days He ate nothing, and afterward, when
they had ended, He was hungry.

3 And the devil said to Him, "If You are the Son of
God, command this stone to become bread."

4 But Jesus answered him, saying, "It is written, 'Man
shall not live by bread alone, but by every word of
God.' "

5 Then the devil, taking Him up on a high mountain,
showed Him all the kingdoms of the world in a
moment of time.

6 And the devil said to Him, "All this authority I will
give You, and their glory; for this has been delivered
to me, and I give it to whomever I wish.

7 Therefore, if You will worship before me, all will be
Yours."

8 And Jesus answered and said to him, "Get behind
Me, Satan! For it is written, 'You shall worship the
LORD your God, and Him only you shall serve.' "

9 Then he brought Him to Jerusalem, set Him on the
pinnacle of the temple, and said to Him, "If You are
the Son of God, throw Yourself down from here.

10 For it is written: 'He shall give His angels charge
over you, To keep you,'

11 and, 'In their hands they shall bear you up, Lest you
dash your foot against a stone.' "

12 And Jesus answered and said to him, "It has been
said, 'You shall not tempt the LORD your God.' "

13 Now when the devil had ended every temptation, he
departed from Him until an opportune time.

tempted for forty days (4:2)—
Evidently the temptation of
Christ encompassed the full
forty days of His fast.

until an opportune time (v. 13)—
Satan's temptations did not end
here for Christ, but persisted
throughout His ministry (see
Hebrews 4:15), culminating in
Gethsemane (Luke 22:39–46).

25

He came to Nazareth (v. 16)—
Verse 23 indicates that Christ
had previously ministered in
Capernaum, another example
of Luke's tendency to order
things logically rather than
chronologically.

the acceptable year of the LORD
(v. 19)—The passage Christ read
was Isaiah 61:1–2. He stopped
in the middle of verse 2. The
rest of the verse prophesies
judgment in the day of God's
vengeance. Since that part of
the verse pertains to the second
advent, Christ did not read it.

this Scripture is fulfilled (v.
21)—Jesus Christ made an un-
ambiguous claim that He was the
Messiah who fulfilled the prophecy. They correctly understood
His meaning but could not ac-
cept such lofty claims from One
whom they knew so well as the
carpenter's son (v. 22).

14 *Then Jesus returned in the power of the Spirit to
Galilee, and news of Him went out through all the
surrounding region.*

15 *And He taught in their synagogues, being glorified
by all.*

16 *So He came to Nazareth, where He had been
brought up. And as His custom was, He went into
the synagogue on the Sabbath day, and stood up to
read.*

17 *And He was handed the book of the prophet Isaiah.
And when He had opened the book, He found the
place where it was written:*

18 *"The Spirit of the LORD is upon Me, Because He has
anointed Me to preach the gospel to the poor; He
has sent Me to heal the brokenhearted, to proclaim
liberty to the captives and recovery of sight to the
blind, to set at liberty those who are oppressed;*

19 *To proclaim the acceptable year of the LORD."*

20 *Then He closed the book, and gave it back to the
attendant and sat down. And the eyes of all who
were in the synagogue were fixed on Him.*

21 *And He began to say to them, "Today this Scripture
is fulfilled in your hearing."*

22 *So all bore witness to Him, and marveled at the
gracious words which proceeded out of His mouth.
And they said, "Is this not Joseph's son?"*

23 *He said to them, "You will surely say this proverb
to Me, 'Physician, heal yourself! Whatever we have
heard done in Capernaum, do also here in Your
country.' "*

24 *Then He said, "Assuredly, I say to you, no prophet is
accepted in his own country.*

25 *But I tell you truly, many widows were in Israel in
the days of Elijah, when the heaven was shut up
three years and six months, and there was a great
famine throughout all the land;*

26 *but to none of them was Elijah sent except to
Zarephath, in the region of Sidon, to a woman who
was a widow.*

27 *And many lepers were in Israel in the time of Elisha the prophet, and none of them was cleansed except Naaman the Syrian."*

28 *So all those in the synagogue, when they heard these things, were filled with wrath,*

29 *and rose up and thrust Him out of the city; and they led Him to the brow of the hill on which their city was built, that they might throw Him down over the cliff.*

30 *Then passing through the midst of them, He went His way.*

31 *Then He went down to Capernaum, a city of Galilee, and was teaching them on the Sabbaths.*

32 *And they were astonished at His teaching, for His word was with authority.*

33 *Now in the synagogue there was a man who had a spirit of an unclean demon. And he cried out with a loud voice,*

34 *saying, "Let us alone! What have we to do with You, Jesus of Nazareth? Did You come to destroy us? I know who You are—the Holy One of God!"*

35 *But Jesus rebuked him, saying, "Be quiet, and come out of him!" And when the demon had thrown him in their midst, it came out of him and did not hurt him.*

36 *Then they were all amazed and spoke among themselves, saying, "What a word this is! For with authority and power He commands the unclean spirits, and they come out."*

37 *And the report about Him went out into every place in the surrounding region.*

38 *Now He arose from the synagogue and entered Simon's house. But Simon's wife's mother was sick with a high fever, and they made request of Him concerning her.*

39 *So He stood over her and rebuked the fever, and it left her. And immediately she arose and served them.*

40 *When the sun was setting, all those who had any*

filled with wrath (v. 28)—Luke's first mention of hostile opposition to Christ's ministry, sparked by Christ's suggestion that divine grace might be withheld from them yet extended to Gentiles

passing through the midst of them (v. 30)—The implication is that this was a miraculous escape—the first of several similar incidents in which He escaped a premature death at the hands of a mob (see John 7:30; 8:59; 10:39).

Holy One of God (v. 34)—Demons always recognized Christ immediately.

Simon's wife's mother (v. 38)—Peter was married (see 1 Cor. 9:5), though no details about his wife are given anywhere in Scripture.

a high fever (v. 38)—Matthew 8:14–15 and Mark 1:30–31 also report this miracle. But only Luke, the physician, remarks that the fever was "high" and makes note of the means Jesus used to heal her (v. 39).

the sun was setting (v. 40)—This signifies the end of the Sabbath. As soon as they were free to travel, the multitudes came.

that were sick with various diseases brought them to
Him; and He laid His hands on every one of them
and healed them.

41 And demons also came out of many, crying out and
saying, "You are the Christ, the Son of God!" And
He, rebuking them, did not allow them to speak, for
they knew that He was the Christ.

42 Now when it was day, He departed and went into
a deserted place. And the crowd sought Him and
came to Him, and tried to keep Him from leaving
them;

kingdom of God (v. 43)—
prominent term throughout the
remainder of Luke's gospel, in-
troduced here for the first time

43 but He said to them, "I must preach the kingdom of
God to the other cities also, because for this purpose
I have been sent."

44 And He was preaching in the synagogues of Galilee.

1) Describe the ministry of John the Baptist—the messenger himself, the
content of his message, his style.

_____

_____

_____

_____

2) What sorts of people came to hear John preach? What was their response
to him?

_____

_____

_____

_____

3) Summarize the things that took place when Christ was baptized.

_____

_____

_____

_____

4) What does Luke 4:1 say about the Spirit's role in Christ's temptation?

_____

_____

_____

5) What happened when Jesus presented Himself as Israel's Messiah in His hometown of Nazareth (4:16–29)?

_____

_____

_____

6) What was the demonic consensus about the identity of Christ (4:34, 41)?

_____

_____

_____

GOING DEEPER

Read John 1:19–34 for additional insight into the ministry and manner of John the Baptist.

19 *Now this is the testimony of John, when the Jews sent priests and Levites from Jerusalem to ask him, "Who are you?"*

20 *He confessed, and did not deny, but confessed, "I am not the Christ."*

21 *And they asked him, "What then? Are you Elijah?" He said, "I am not." "Are you the Prophet?" And he answered, "No."*

22 *Then they said to him, "Who are you, that we may give an answer to those who sent us? What do you say about yourself?"*

23 *He said: "I am 'The voice of one crying in the wilderness: "Make straight the way of the LORD," ' as the prophet Isaiah said."*

24 *Now those who were sent were from the Pharisees.*

25 *And they asked him, saying, "Why then do you baptize if you are not the Christ, nor Elijah, nor the Prophet?"*

26 *John answered them, saying, "I baptize with water, but there stands One among you whom you do not know.*

27 *It is He who, coming after me, is preferred before me, whose sandal strap I am not worthy to loose."*

28 *These things were done in Bethabara beyond the Jordan, where John was baptizing.*

29 *The next day John saw Jesus coming toward him, and said, "Behold! The Lamb of God who takes away the sin of the world!*

30 *This is He of whom I said, 'After me comes a Man who is preferred before me, for He was before me.'*

31 *I did not know Him; but that He should be revealed to Israel, therefore I came baptizing with water."*

32 *And John bore witness, saying, "I saw the Spirit descending from heaven like a dove, and He remained upon Him.*

33 *I did not know Him, but He who sent me to baptize with water said to me, 'Upon whom you see the Spirit descending, and remaining on Him, this is He who baptizes with the Holy Spirit.'*

34 *And I have seen and testified that this is the Son of God."*

EXPLORING THE MEANING

7) How does the apostle John's record of John the Baptist add to your understanding of what his purpose was as the forerunner to the Messiah?

8) Modalism is a theological heresy that suggests that God is one person who manifests Himself in three distinct modes, one at a time. How does Luke's account of the baptism of Jesus refute the error of modalism?

9) In the temptation account, Jesus quotes Deuteronomy 8:3 (4:4), then Deuteronomy 6:13 (v. 8). After Satan quotes Psalm 91:11–12 (vv. 10–11), Christ quotes Deuteronomy 6:16. What principles do you see here about temptation, the devil, and knowing Scripture?

10) If you had been a first-person witness to these events, what conclusions would you have come to about Jesus' identity, message, and mission?

_____

_____

_____

_____

_____

TRUTH FOR TODAY

How can you enhance your passion for the lost? First, study Christ's great love, compassion, and tender mercy. You can study great men and women in church history, but ultimately you must understand the heart of Jesus. As 1 John 2:6 says, "He who says he abides in Him ought himself also to walk just as He walked" (NKJV).

Second, study sin: its guilt, power, and penalty. That will make you aware of how we have all fallen prey to the subtleties of the world. Romans 12:2 says, "Do not be conformed to this world, but be transformed by the renewing of your mind" (NKJV). Let it remind you to be preoccupied not with worldly things, but with evangelizing the lost.

Third, study sinners. Try to cultivate love and sympathy for them, not bitterness. Note that the most zealous evangelists are often new converts.

Fourth, study Scripture. See what it says about hell, death, judgment, and salvation.

And finally, pray for God to give you a passion for evangelism.

REFLECTING ON THE TEXT

11) Christ was clearly "on a mission." In His desire to see God glorified, Jesus demonstrated compassion to a lost humanity, healing, teaching, proclaiming the Good News. On a scale of 1–10, how would you rate your desire to reach out to others?

_____

_____

_____

_____

12) Temptation is a fact of life in a fallen world. With Christ as your perfect example, what can and will you do today to resist Satan's schemes?

_____

_____

_____

13) Many unbelievers have an unfavorable view of Christ. What "favorable facts" about Jesus do you see in these two chapters of Luke's gospel?

_____

_____

_____

Personal Response

Write out additional reflections, questions you may have, or a prayer.

_____

_____

_____

_____

_____

_____

_____

_____

_____

_____

_____

_____

_____

_____

_____

~3~
CHRIST'S DISCIPLES

DRAWING NEAR

What leader (pastor, political figure, teacher, coach, etc.) has impacted your life in a lasting way? What made you want to "follow" or be around this person?

_____

_____

_____

_____

_____

_____

_____

THE CONTEXT

Writing to set forth "an orderly account" of the extraordinary life of Jesus Christ, Luke continues his description of the Son of Man's ministry in Galilee. Primarily these chapters record Christ's calling of the twelve men who are first identified as disciples, and later as apostles. How amazing that this unlikely band of followers will become the human leaders of the worldwide entity known as the church! Not only does the Son of Man demonstrate authority over men in this portion of Luke's gospel, but He also shows sovereign authority over nature, disease and defilement, sin and its consequences, and religious tradition.

KEYS TO THE TEXT

Apostles: This term means "messengers, sent ones," and is from the Greek word *apostoloi.* Luke reserves the term almost exclusively for the twelve disciples who were specifically called to a unique office of authority in Christ. The role of an apostle involved a position of leadership and exclusive teaching authority in the early church. The New Testament Scriptures were all written by the apostles or their close associates. And before the New Testament was written, the apostles' teaching was the rule in the early church.

UNLEASHING THE TEXT

Read 5:1–6:16, noting the key words and definitions next to the passage.

Luke 5:1–6:16 (NKJV)

Lake of Gennesaret (v. 1)—i.e., the Sea of Galilee, actually a large freshwater lake, over 690 feet below sea level, and the main source of water and commerce for the Galilee region

1 *So it was, as the multitude pressed about Him to hear the word of God, that He stood by the Lake of Gennesaret,*

2 *and saw two boats standing by the lake; but the fishermen had gone from them and were washing their nets.*

3 *Then He got into one of the boats, which was Simon's, and asked him to put out a little from the land. And He sat down and taught the multitudes from the boat.*

let down your nets (v. 4)— Normally, the fish that were netted in shallow water at night would migrate during the daylight hours to waters too deep to reach easily with nets, which is why Peter fished at night.

4 *When He had stopped speaking, He said to Simon, "Launch out into the deep and let down your nets for a catch."*

5 *But Simon answered and said to Him, "Master, we have toiled all night and caught nothing; nevertheless at Your word I will let down the net."*

6 *And when they had done this, they caught a great number of fish, and their net was breaking.*

7 *So they signaled to their partners in the other boat to come and help them. And they came and filled both the boats, so that they began to sink.*

Depart from me (v. 8)—This remarkable catch of fish was clearly a miracle, and Peter realized he was in the presence of the Holy One.

8 *When Simon Peter saw it, he fell down at Jesus' knees, saying, "Depart from me, for I am a sinful man, O Lord!"*

9 *For he and all who were with him were astonished at the catch of fish which they had taken;*

10 *and so also were James and John, the sons of Zebedee, who were partners with Simon. And Jesus said to Simon, "Do not be afraid. From now on you will catch men."*

11 *So when they had brought their boats to land, they forsook all and followed Him.*

full of leprosy (v. 12)—an extremely serious case

12 *And it happened when He was in a certain city, that behold, a man who was full of leprosy saw Jesus; and he fell on his face and implored Him, saying,*

"Lord, if You are willing, You can make me clean."

13 Then He put out His hand and touched him, saying, "I am willing; be cleansed." Immediately the leprosy left him.

14 And He charged him to tell no one, "But go and show yourself to the priest, and make an offering for your cleansing, as a testimony to them, just as Moses commanded."

show yourself to the priest (v. 14)—in accordance with the law governing leprosy (Lev. 13:1–46)

15 However, the report went around concerning Him all the more; and great multitudes came together to hear, and to be healed by Him of their infirmities.

16 So He Himself often withdrew into the wilderness and prayed.

17 Now it happened on a certain day, as He was teaching, that there were Pharisees and teachers of the law sitting by, who had come out of every town of Galilee, Judea, and Jerusalem. And the power of the Lord was present to heal them.

18 Then behold, men brought on a bed a man who was paralyzed, whom they sought to bring in and lay before Him.

19 And when they could not find how they might bring him in, because of the crowd, they went up on the housetop and let him down with his bed through the tiling into the midst before Jesus.

through the tiling (v. 19)—apparently a wealthy person's home, built in the Greco-Roman style, with roof tiles that, when removed, gave access to lower the man between the roof beams

20 When He saw their faith, He said to him, "Man, your sins are forgiven you."

21 And the scribes and the Pharisees began to reason, saying, "Who is this who speaks blasphemies? Who can forgive sins but God alone?"

perceived (v. 22)—i.e., by means of His omniscience (see Matt. 9:4; John 5:24–25)

22 But when Jesus perceived their thoughts, He answered and said to them, "Why are you reasoning in your hearts?

23 Which is easier, to say, 'Your sins are forgiven you,' or to say, 'Rise up and walk'?

24 But that you may know that the Son of Man has power on earth to forgive sins"—He said to the man who was paralyzed, "I say to you, arise, take up your bed, and go to your house."

that you may know. (v. 22)—Christ's ability to heal anyone and everyone at will—totally and immediately (v. 25)—was incontrovertible proof of His deity. As God, He had all authority to forgive sins. This was a decisive moment and should have ended once and for all the Pharisees' opposition. Instead, they began to try to discredit Him by charging Him with violating their Sabbath rules.

strange things (v. 26)—The
men's response is curiously non-
committal—not void of wonder
and amazement, but utterly void
of true faith.

25 *Immediately he rose up before them, took up what
he had been lying on, and departed to his own
house, glorifying God.*

26 *And they were all amazed, and they glorified God
and were filled with fear, saying, "We have seen
strange things today!"*

27 *After these things He went out and saw a tax
collector named Levi, sitting at the tax office. And
He said to him, "Follow Me."*

28 *So he left all, rose up, and followed Him.*

29 *Then Levi gave Him a great feast in his own house.
And there were a great number of tax collectors and
others who sat down with them.*

30 *And their scribes and the Pharisees complained
against His disciples, saying, "Why do You eat and
drink with tax collectors and sinners?"*

who are well (v. 31)—I.e., those
who think they are whole don't
seek healing.

31 *Jesus answered and said to them, "Those who are
well have no need of a physician, but those who are
sick.*

32 *I have not come to call the righteous, but sinners, to
repentance."*

33 *Then they said to Him, "Why do the disciples of
John fast often and make prayers, and likewise
those of the Pharisees, but Yours eat and drink?"*

fast often (v. 33)—Jesus fasted
privately on at least one occasion (Matt. 4:2); the Law
prescribed a fast on the Day
of Atonement (Lev. 16:29–31;
23:27)—all other fasts were supposed to be voluntary, for specific reasons such as penitence
and earnest prayer. The fact that
the Pharisees raised this question shows that they thought
of fasting as a public exercise to
display one's own spirituality.

34 *And He said to them, "Can you make the friends of
the bridegroom fast while the bridegroom is with
them?*

35 *But the days will come when the bridegroom will be
taken away from them; then they will fast in those
days."*

36 *Then He spoke a parable to them: "No one puts a
piece from a new garment on an old one; otherwise
the new makes a tear, and also the piece that was
taken out of the new does not match the old.*

37 *And no one puts new wine into old wineskins; or
else the new wine will burst the wineskins and be
spilled, and the wineskins will be ruined.*

38 *But new wine must be put into new wineskins, and
both are preserved.*

39 *And no one, having drunk old wine, immediately desires new; for he says, 'The old is better.' "*

6:1 *Now it happened on the second Sabbath after the first that He went through the grainfields. And His disciples plucked the heads of grain and ate them, rubbing them in their hands.*

2 *And some of the Pharisees said to them, "Why are you doing what is not lawful to do on the Sabbath?"*

3 *But Jesus answering them said, "Have you not even read this, what David did when he was hungry, he and those who were with him:*

4 *how he went into the house of God, took and ate the showbread, and also gave some to those with him, which is not lawful for any but the priests to eat?"*

5 *And He said to them, "The Son of Man is also Lord of the Sabbath."*

6 *Now it happened on another Sabbath, also, that He entered the synagogue and taught. And a man was there whose right hand was withered.*

7 *So the scribes and Pharisees watched Him closely, whether He would heal on the Sabbath, that they might find an accusation against Him.*

8 *But He knew their thoughts, and said to the man who had the withered hand, "Arise and stand here." And he arose and stood.*

9 *Then Jesus said to them, "I will ask you one thing: Is it lawful on the Sabbath to do good or to do evil, to save life or to destroy?"*

10 *And when He had looked around at them all, He said to the man, "Stretch out your hand." And he did so, and his hand was restored as whole as the other.*

11 *But they were filled with rage, and discussed with one another what they might do to Jesus.*

12 *Now it came to pass in those days that He went out to the mountain to pray, and continued all night in prayer to God.*

13 *And when it was day, He called His disciples to Himself; and from them He chose twelve whom He also named apostles:*

'The old is better.' (v. 39)—Those who had acquired a taste for Old Covenant ceremonies and Pharisaic traditions were loath to give them up for the new wine of Jesus' teaching.

whether He would heal on the Sabbath (6:7)—The scribes and Pharisees spotted the man with the withered hand (v. 6), and, with Christ present, they immediately knew that this would be an occasion for the man's healing. In stark contrast to all other so-called healers, Christ was not selective. He healed all who came to Him (v. 19; see 4:40; Matt. 8:16).

to do good (v. 9)—The Sabbath laws prohibited labor for profit, frivolous diversions, and things extraneous to worship, but good works were appropriate on the Sabbath—particularly deeds of charity, mercy, worship, and the preservation of life. To corrupt the Sabbath to forbid such works was a perversion of God's design.

He called His disciples (v. 13)—Christ had many disciples, at one point sending seventy out in pairs to proclaim the gospel (10:1), but on this occasion, He chose twelve and specifically commissioned them as apostles, i.e., "sent ones," with a special authority to deliver His message.

14 *Simon, whom He also named Peter, and Andrew his brother; James and John; Philip and Bartholomew;*

15 *Matthew and Thomas; James the son of Alphaeus, and Simon called the Zealot;*

16 *Judas the son of James, and Judas Iscariot who also became a traitor.*

1) Describe what happened when Christ called Simon (Peter), Andrew, James, and John. What did Jesus ask Peter to do, and what was his response?

_____

_____

_____

_____

2) Christ, when confronted with a paralyzed man, responded in an unexpected way. What do His words and actions say about His identity?

_____

_____

_____

3) Why would the events of Luke 5:27–32 have raised eyebrows and stirred up the religious leaders?

_____

_____

_____

4) Summarize the interchange between Jesus and the Jewish leaders in Luke 5:33–39. What was each party saying or suggesting?

_____

_____

_____

5) Luke 6:1–11 focuses on a couple of incidents that happened on the Jewish Sabbath. What did Jesus do here, and what was the response of the religious leaders?

_____

_____

_____

_____

6) List the men Jesus chose to be His followers. Compare Luke's list with Mark 3:13–19. Do any of the Twelve go by other names?

_____

_____

_____

_____

GOING DEEPER

Read Matthew 9:9–13 for another account of the calling of Matthew.

9 *As Jesus passed on from there, He saw a man named Matthew sitting at the tax office. And He said to him, "Follow Me." So he arose and followed Him.*

10 *Now it happened, as Jesus sat at the table in the house, that behold, many tax collectors and sinners came and sat down with Him and His disciples.*

11 *And when the Pharisees saw it, they said to His disciples, "Why does your Teacher eat with tax collectors and sinners?"*

12 *When Jesus heard that, He said to them, "Those who are well have no need of a physician, but those who are sick.*

13 *But go and learn what this means: 'I desire mercy and not sacrifice.' For I did not come to call the righteous, but sinners, to repentance."*

EXPLORING THE MEANING

7) Upon meeting Christ, what was Levi's (Matthew's) immediate response?

_____

_____

8) Why did Jesus' actions create such a scandal among the religious elite? How did rabbis typically view and treat "tax collectors and sinners"?

_____

_____

_____

_____

9) What was Christ saying or revealing about Himself in the healing of the paralytic (5:17–26)?

_____

_____

_____

_____

10) When Jesus healed the man with the withered hand, the scribes and Pharisees were "filled with rage" (6:11 NKJV). This is a curious response in the face of so glorious a miracle. What was behind their blind fury?

_____

_____

_____

_____

11) Prior to choosing His twelve disciples, Luke 6:12 says that Jesus "continued all night in prayer" (NKJV). Why is this significant? What does this fact tell you about Jesus?

_____

_____

_____

_____

Truth for Today

Think about the ramifications of this fact. From our human perspective, the propagation of the gospel and the founding of the church hinged entirely on twelve men whose most outstanding characteristic was their ordinariness. They were chosen by Christ and trained for a time that is best measured in months, not years. He taught them the Scriptures and theology. He discipled them in the ways of godly living (teaching them and showing them how to pray, how to forgive, and how to serve one another with humility). He gave them moral instruction. He spoke to them of things to come. And He employed them as His instruments to heal the sick, cast out demons, and do other miraculous works. Empowered by the Holy Spirit at Pentecost, they valiantly undertook the task to which Jesus had called them. The work they subsequently began continues today, two thousand years later. They are living proof that God's strength is made perfect in weakness.

REFLECTING ON THE TEXT

12) How are you personally encouraged by the truth that the original twelve followers of Jesus—who were quirky, inconsistent, and slow to grasp the implications of the gospel—became men who changed the world?

_____

_____

_____

_____

13) What new insight(s) do you find in these chapters about the Person and work of Jesus Christ?

_____

_____

_____

_____

14) Despite His holy nature, Christ was obviously welcomed by "sinners." They did not avoid Him. On the contrary, they sought Him out. Why is it so rare for modern-day sinners to be drawn to the followers of Christ? What can you do to be a more winsome witness?

_____

_____

_____

_____

Personal Response

Write out additional reflections, questions you may have, or a prayer.

_____

_____

_____

_____

_____

_____

_____

_____

_____

_____

_____

_____

_____

_____

_____

_____

_____

_____

_____

_____

_____

_____

_____

_____

_____

_____

~4~
CHRIST'S MESSAGE, MINISTRY, AND MIRACLES

Luke 6:17–9:50

DRAWING NEAR

Jesus' ministry was full of wonderful teaching and miracles. His ministry goes on today in our lives too. Think back over your recent spiritual journey. Then describe a time when:

⟶ You were deeply convicted by a truth from God's Word.

_____

_____

_____

_____

⟶ You participated in a vital ministry and felt that God used you.

_____

_____

_____

⟶ You experienced God's supernatural touch (e.g., you experienced some kind of physical healing, or you enjoyed victory over a sinful habit, or you received illumination regarding some life-changing truth, etc.).

_____

_____

_____

_____

THE CONTEXT

These next chapters in Luke record Christ's preaching, healing, and teaching. Beginning in 6:17, we find the so-called Sermon on the Plateau. The similarity to the Sermon on the Mount (Matt. 5:1–7:29) is remarkable. It is possible, of course, that Jesus simply preached the same sermon on more than one occasion. It appears more likely, however, that these are variant accounts of the same event. Luke's version is abbreviated somewhat, because—writing to a Gentile audience—he omitted sections from the sermon that are uniquely Jewish.

Chapter 7 spotlights Christ's mercy and kindness. He performs two miracles: the healing of a Roman centurion's servant and the raising of a widow's son. In chapter 8, Christ begins to speak to the masses in parables. His veiling of truth from unbelievers was both an act of judgment and an act of mercy. Chapter 9 documents Christ's training of the Twelve, the Transfiguration, and some stern words about discipleship.

KEYS TO THE TEXT

Gospel: Literally, this word means "good news" or "good message," from the Greek word *euangelion.* Messengers bringing news of victory in battle originally used this Greek term. In the New Testament it points to the good news of salvation, which is: Jesus Christ came to earth to abolish the power of sin in the lives of His people by offering Himself as a perfect sacrifice on the cross. Christ commands believers to share this gospel with the rest of the world. This good news is Christ's life-giving message to a dying world.

UNLEASHING THE TEXT

Read 6:17–9:50, noting the key words and definitions next to the passage.

Luke 6:17–9:50 (NKJV)

unclean spirits (v. 18)—another name for demons, used ten times in the Gospels

you poor (v. 20)—Christ's concern for the poor and outcasts is one of Luke's favorite themes; the poverty spoken of here refers primarily to a sense of one's own spiritual impoverishment.

you who hunger (v. 21)—no mere craving for food, but a spiritual hunger and thirst for righteousness

For the Son of Man's sake (v. 22)—Persecution per se is not something to be sought, but when evil is spoken against a Christian falsely and for Christ's sake, such persecution carries with it the blessing of God.

17 And He came down with them and stood on a level place with a crowd of His disciples and a great multitude of people from all Judea and Jerusalem, and from the seacoast of Tyre and Sidon, who came to hear Him and be healed of their diseases,

18 as well as those who were tormented with unclean spirits. And they were healed.

19 And the whole multitude sought to touch Him, for power went out from Him and healed them all.

20 Then He lifted up His eyes toward His disciples, and said: "Blessed are you poor, for yours is the kingdom of God.

21 Blessed are you who hunger now, for you shall be filled. Blessed are you who weep now, for you shall laugh.

22 Blessed are you when men hate you, and when they exclude you, and revile you, and cast out your name as evil, for the Son of Man's sake.

23 *Rejoice in that day and leap for joy! For indeed your reward is great in heaven, for in like manner their fathers did to the prophets.*

24 *"But woe to you who are rich, for you have received your consolation.*

25 *Woe to you who are full, for you shall hunger. Woe to you who laugh now, for you shall mourn and weep.*

26 *Woe to you when all men speak well of you, for so did their fathers to the false prophets.*

27 *"But I say to you who hear: Love your enemies, do good to those who hate you,*

28 *bless those who curse you, and pray for those who spitefully use you.*

29 *To him who strikes you on the one cheek, offer the other also. And from him who takes away your cloak, do not withhold your tunic either.*

30 *Give to everyone who asks of you. And from him who takes away your goods do not ask them back.*

31 *And just as you want men to do to you, you also do to them likewise.*

32 *"But if you love those who love you, what credit is that to you? For even sinners love those who love them.*

33 *And if you do good to those who do good to you, what credit is that to you? For even sinners do the same.*

34 *And if you lend to those from whom you hope to receive back, what credit is that to you? For even sinners lend to sinners to receive as much back.*

35 *But love your enemies, do good, and lend, hoping for nothing in return; and your reward will be great, and you will be sons of the Most High. For He is kind to the unthankful and evil.*

36 *Therefore be merciful, just as your Father also is merciful.*

37 *"Judge not, and you shall not be judged. Condemn not, and you shall not be condemned. Forgive, and you will be forgiven.*

sons of the Most High (v. 35)—God's children should bear the indelible stamp of His moral character—love, grace, and generosity—even to those who are His enemies.

Judge not (v. 37)—This command forbids hypocrisy and a condemning spirit rising from self-righteousness; it does not condemn true discernment.

speck . . . plank (v. 41)—The humor of the imagery was no doubt intentional; Christ often employed hyperbole to paint comical images (see 18:25; Matt. 23:24).

you call Me 'Lord, Lord.' (v. 46)—It is not sufficient to give lip service to Christ's lordship. Genuine faith produces obedience. A tree is known by its fruits (v. 44).

38 *Give, and it will be given to you: good measure, pressed down, shaken together, and running over will be put into your bosom. For with the same measure that you use, it will be measured back to you."*

39 *And He spoke a parable to them: "Can the blind lead the blind? Will they not both fall into the ditch?*

40 *A disciple is not above his teacher, but everyone who is perfectly trained will be like his teacher.*

41 *And why do you look at the speck in your brother's eye, but do not perceive the plank in your own eye?*

42 *Or how can you say to your brother, 'Brother, let me remove the speck that is in your eye,' when you yourself do not see the plank that is in your own eye? Hypocrite! First remove the plank from your own eye, and then you will see clearly to remove the speck that is in your brother's eye.*

43 *"For a good tree does not bear bad fruit, nor does a bad tree bear good fruit.*

44 *For every tree is known by its own fruit. For men do not gather figs from thorns, nor do they gather grapes from a bramble bush.*

45 *A good man out of the good treasure of his heart brings forth good; and an evil man out of the evil treasure of his heart brings forth evil. For out of the abundance of the heart his mouth speaks.*

46 *"But why do you call Me 'Lord, Lord,' and not do the things which I say?*

47 *Whoever comes to Me, and hears My sayings and does them, I will show you whom he is like:*

48 *He is like a man building a house, who dug deep and laid the foundation on the rock. And when the flood arose, the stream beat vehemently against that house, and could not shake it, for it was founded on the rock.*

49 *But he who heard and did nothing is like a man who built a house on the earth without a foundation, against which the stream beat vehemently; and immediately it fell. And the ruin of that house was great."*

7:1 *Now when He concluded all His sayings in the hearing of the people, He entered Capernaum.*

2 *And a certain centurion's servant, who was dear to him, was sick and ready to die.*

3 *So when he heard about Jesus, he sent elders of the Jews to Him, pleading with Him to come and heal his servant.*

4 *And when they came to Jesus, they begged Him earnestly, saying that the one for whom He should do this was deserving,*

5 *"for he loves our nation, and has built us a synagogue."*

6 *Then Jesus went with them. And when He was already not far from the house, the centurion sent friends to Him, saying to Him, "Lord, do not trouble Yourself, for I am not worthy that You should enter under my roof.*

7 *Therefore I did not even think myself worthy to come to You. But say the word, and my servant will be healed.*

8 *For I also am a man placed under authority, having soldiers under me. And I say to one, 'Go,' and he goes; and to another, 'Come,' and he comes; and to my servant, 'Do this,' and he does it."*

9 *When Jesus heard these things, He marveled at him, and turned around and said to the crowd that followed Him, "I say to you, I have not found such great faith, not even in Israel!"*

10 *And those who were sent, returning to the house, found the servant well who had been sick.*

11 *Now it happened, the day after, that He went into a city called Nain; and many of His disciples went with Him, and a large crowd.*

12 *And when He came near the gate of the city, behold, a dead man was being carried out, the only son of his mother; and she was a widow. And a large crowd from the city was with her.*

13 *When the Lord saw her, He had compassion on her and said to her, "Do not weep."*

centurion's servant (7:2)—one of three centurions featured in the New Testament who gave evidence of genuine faith

Nain (v. 11)—a small town southeast of Nazareth

touched the open coffin (v. 14)— A ceremonially defiling act, normally, but Jesus graphically illustrated how impervious He was to such defilements.

14 Then He came and touched the open coffin, and those who carried him stood still. And He said, "Young man, I say to you, arise."

15 So he who was dead sat up and began to speak. And He presented him to his mother.

16 Then fear came upon all, and they glorified God, saying, "A great prophet has risen up among us"; and, "God has visited His people."

17 And this report about Him went throughout all Judea and all the surrounding region.

18 Then the disciples of John reported to him concerning all these things.

19 And John, calling two of his disciples to him, sent them to Jesus, saying, "Are You the Coming One, or do we look for another?"

20 When the men had come to Him, they said, "John the Baptist has sent us to You, saying, 'Are You the Coming One, or do we look for another?'"

21 And that very hour He cured many of infirmities, afflictions, and evil spirits; and to many blind He gave sight.

22 Jesus answered and said to them, "Go and tell John the things you have seen and heard: that the blind see, the lame walk, the lepers are cleansed, the deaf hear, the dead are raised, the poor have the gospel preached to them.

23 And blessed is he who is not offended because of Me."

24 When the messengers of John had departed, He began to speak to the multitudes concerning John: "What did you go out into the wilderness to see? A reed shaken by the wind?

25 But what did you go out to see? A man clothed in soft garments? Indeed those who are gorgeously appareled and live in luxury are in kings' courts.

26 But what did you go out to see? A prophet? Yes, I say to you, and more than a prophet.

27 This is he of whom it is written: 'Behold, I send My messenger before Your face, who will prepare Your way before You.'

28 *For I say to you, among those born of women there is not a greater prophet than John the Baptist; but he who is least in the kingdom of God is greater than he."*

29 *And when all the people heard Him, even the tax collectors justified God, having been baptized with the baptism of John.*

30 *But the Pharisees and lawyers rejected the will of God for themselves, not having been baptized by him.*

31 *And the Lord said, "To what then shall I liken the men of this generation, and what are they like?*

32 *They are like children sitting in the marketplace and calling to one another, saying: 'We played the flute for you, And you did not dance; We mourned to you, And you did not weep.'*

33 *For John the Baptist came neither eating bread nor drinking wine, and you say, 'He has a demon.'*

34 *The Son of Man has come eating and drinking, and you say, 'Look, a glutton and a winebibber, a friend of tax collectors and sinners!'*

35 *But wisdom is justified by all her children."*

36 *Then one of the Pharisees asked Him to eat with him. And He went to the Pharisee's house, and sat down to eat.*

37 *And behold, a woman in the city who was a sinner, when she knew that Jesus sat at the table in the Pharisee's house, brought an alabaster flask of fragrant oil,*

38 *and stood at His feet behind Him weeping; and she began to wash His feet with her tears, and wiped them with the hair of her head; and she kissed His feet and anointed them with the fragrant oil.*

39 *Now when the Pharisee who had invited Him saw this, he spoke to himself, saying, "This Man, if He were a prophet, would know who and what manner of woman this is who is touching Him, for she is a sinner."*

40 *And Jesus answered and said to him, "Simon, I have something to say to you." So he said, "Teacher, say it."*

rejected the will of God (v. 30)—John's call to repentance was an expression of the will of God. By refusing repentance, they rejected God Himself.

like children (v. 32)—Rebuking the Pharisees, Christ suggested they were behaving childishly, determined not to be pleased, whether invited to "dance" (a reference to Christ's joyous style of ministry, "eating and drinking" with sinners—v. 34) or urged to "weep" (a reference to John the Baptist's call to repentance, and John's more austere manner of ministry—v. 33).

wisdom is justified by all her children (v. 35)—In other words, true wisdom is vindicated by its consequences—what it produces (see James 2:14–17).

an alabaster flask (v. 37)—This was similar to the anointing that Mary, sister of Martha and Lazarus, performed in Bethany, during Passion Week (Matt. 26:6–13; Mark 14:3–9; John 12:2–8), but clearly a different incident. This incident takes place in Galilee and involves "a woman . . . who was a sinner"—i.e., a prostitute. There is no reason to identify this woman with Mary Magdalene, as some have done.

what manner of woman (v. 39)—The Pharisees showed nothing but contempt for sinners.

no water for My feet (v. 44)—
This glaring oversight was tantamount to an insult. Washing a guest's feet was an essential formality.

Your faith has saved you (v. 50)—Not all whom Jesus healed were saved, but those who exhibited true faith were.

certain women (8:2)—Rabbis normally did not have women as disciples.

41 "There was a certain creditor who had two debtors. One owed five hundred denarii, and the other fifty.

42 And when they had nothing with which to repay, he freely forgave them both. Tell Me, therefore, which of them will love him more?"

43 Simon answered and said, "I suppose the one whom he forgave more." And He said to him, "You have rightly judged."

44 Then He turned to the woman and said to Simon, "Do you see this woman? I entered your house; you gave Me no water for My feet, but she has washed My feet with her tears and wiped them with the hair of her head.

45 You gave Me no kiss, but this woman has not ceased to kiss My feet since the time I came in.

46 You did not anoint My head with oil, but this woman has anointed My feet with fragrant oil.

47 Therefore I say to you, her sins, which are many, are forgiven, for she loved much. But to whom little is forgiven, the same loves little."

48 Then He said to her, "Your sins are forgiven."

49 And those who sat at the table with Him began to say to themselves, "Who is this who even forgives sins?"

50 Then He said to the woman, "Your faith has saved you. Go in peace."

8:1 Now it came to pass, afterward, that He went through every city and village, preaching and bringing the glad tidings of the kingdom of God. And the twelve were with Him,

2 and certain women who had been healed of evil spirits and infirmities—Mary called Magdalene, out of whom had come seven demons,

3 and Joanna the wife of Chuza, Herod's steward, and Susanna, and many others who provided for Him from their substance.

4 And when a great multitude had gathered, and they had come to Him from every city, He spoke by a parable:

5 "A sower went out to sow his seed. And as he sowed, some fell by the wayside; and it was trampled down, and the birds of the air devoured it.

6 Some fell on rock; and as soon as it sprang up, it withered away because it lacked moisture.

7 And some fell among thorns, and the thorns sprang up with it and choked it.

8 But others fell on good ground, sprang up, and yielded a crop a hundredfold." When He had said these things He cried, "He who has ears to hear, let him hear!"

9 Then His disciples asked Him, saying, "What does this parable mean?"

10 And He said, "To you it has been given to know the mysteries of the kingdom of God, but to the rest it is given in parables, that 'Seeing they may not see, And hearing they may not understand.'

11 "Now the parable is this: The seed is the word of God.

12 Those by the wayside are the ones who hear; then the devil comes and takes away the word out of their hearts, lest they should believe and be saved.

13 But the ones on the rock are those who, when they hear, receive the word with joy; and these have no root, who believe for a while and in time of temptation fall away.

14 Now the ones that fell among thorns are those who, when they have heard, go out and are choked with cares, riches, and pleasures of life, and bring no fruit to maturity.

15 But the ones that fell on the good ground are those who, having heard the word with a noble and good heart, keep it and bear fruit with patience.

16 "No one, when he has lit a lamp, covers it with a vessel or puts it under a bed, but sets it on a lampstand, that those who enter may see the light.

17 For nothing is secret that will not be revealed, nor anything hidden that will not be known and come to light.

on rock (v. 6)—i.e., very shallow soil with a layer of rock lying just below the surface; perhaps a reference to the fickle mob that followed Jesus only for His miracles

Seeing they may not see (v. 10)—This quotation from Isaiah 6:9 describes God's act of judicially blinding unbelievers.

who believe for a while (v. 13)—i.e., a nominal, nonsaving faith

under a bed (v. 16)—The fact that Christ taught mysteries in parables was not to suggest that His message was meant for elite disciples or that it should be kept secret; still, only those with eyes to see will see it.

18 *Therefore take heed how you hear. For whoever has, to him more will be given; and whoever does not have, even what he seems to have will be taken from him."*

19 *Then His mother and brothers came to Him, and could not approach Him because of the crowd.*

20 *And it was told Him by some, who said, "Your mother and Your brothers are standing outside, desiring to see You."*

21 *But He answered and said to them, "My mother and My brothers are these who hear the word of God and do it."*

22 *Now it happened, on a certain day, that He got into a boat with His disciples. And He said to them, "Let us cross over to the other side of the lake." And they launched out.*

23 *But as they sailed He fell asleep. And a windstorm came down on the lake, and they were filling with water, and were in jeopardy.*

24 *And they came to Him and awoke Him, saying, "Master, Master, we are perishing!" Then He arose and rebuked the wind and the raging of the water. And they ceased, and there was a calm.*

25 *But He said to them, "Where is your faith?" And they were afraid, and marveled, saying to one another, "Who can this be? For He commands even the winds and water, and they obey Him!"*

26 *Then they sailed to the country of the Gadarenes, which is opposite Galilee.*

27 *And when He stepped out on the land, there met Him a certain man from the city who had demons for a long time. And he wore no clothes, nor did he live in a house but in the tombs.*

28 *When he saw Jesus, he cried out, fell down before Him, and with a loud voice said, "What have I to do with You, Jesus, Son of the Most High God? I beg You, do not torment me!"*

29 *For He had commanded the unclean spirit to come out of the man. For it had often seized him, and*

*he was kept under guard, bound with chains and
shackles; and he broke the bonds and was driven by
the demon into the wilderness.*

30 *Jesus asked him, saying, "What is your name?"
And he said, "Legion," because many demons had
entered him.*

31 *And they begged Him that He would not command
them to go out into the abyss.*

32 *Now a herd of many swine was feeding there on
the mountain. So they begged Him that He would
permit them to enter them. And He permitted
them.*

33 *Then the demons went out of the man and entered
the swine, and the herd ran violently down the steep
place into the lake and drowned.*

34 *When those who fed them saw what had happened,
they fled and told it in the city and in the country.*

35 *Then they went out to see what had happened, and
came to Jesus, and found the man from whom the
demons had departed, sitting at the feet of Jesus,
clothed and in his right mind. And they were afraid.*

36 *They also who had seen it told them by what means
he who had been demon-possessed was healed.*

37 *Then the whole multitude of the surrounding region
of the Gadarenes asked Him to depart from them,
for they were seized with great fear. And He got into
the boat and returned.*

38 *Now the man from whom the demons had departed
begged Him that he might be with Him. But Jesus
sent him away, saying,*

39 *"Return to your own house, and tell what great
things God has done for you." And he went his way
and proclaimed throughout the whole city what
great things Jesus had done for him.*

40 *So it was, when Jesus returned, that the multitude
welcomed Him, for they were all waiting for Him.*

41 *And behold, there came a man named Jairus, and
he was a ruler of the synagogue. And he fell down
at Jesus' feet and begged Him to come to his house,*

42 for he had an only daughter about twelve years of age, and she was dying. But as He went, the multitudes thronged Him.

43 Now a woman, having a flow of blood for twelve years, who had spent all her livelihood on physicians and could not be healed by any,

44 came from behind and touched the border of His garment. And immediately her flow of blood stopped.

45 And Jesus said, "Who touched Me?" When all denied it, Peter and those with him said, "Master, the multitudes throng and press You, and You say, 'Who touched Me?' "

46 But Jesus said, "Somebody touched Me, for I perceived power going out from Me."

47 Now when the woman saw that she was not hidden, she came trembling; and falling down before Him, she declared to Him in the presence of all the people the reason she had touched Him and how she was healed immediately.

48 And He said to her, "Daughter, be of good cheer; your faith has made you well. Go in peace."

49 While He was still speaking, someone came from the ruler of the synagogue's house, saying to him, "Your daughter is dead. Do not trouble the Teacher."

50 But when Jesus heard it, He answered him, saying, "Do not be afraid; only believe, and she will be made well."

51 When He came into the house, He permitted no one to go in except Peter, James, and John, and the father and mother of the girl.

52 Now all wept and mourned for her; but He said, "Do not weep; she is not dead, but sleeping."

53 And they ridiculed Him, knowing that she was dead.

54 But He put them all outside, took her by the hand and called, saying, "Little girl, arise."

55 Then her spirit returned, and she arose immediately. And He commanded that she be given something to eat.

56 *And her parents were astonished, but He charged them to tell no one what had happened.*

9:1 *Then He called His twelve disciples together and gave them power and authority over all demons, and to cure diseases.*

2 *He sent them to preach the kingdom of God and to heal the sick.*

3 *And He said to them, "Take nothing for the journey, neither staffs nor bag nor bread nor money; and do not have two tunics apiece.*

4 *"Whatever house you enter, stay there, and from there depart.*

5 *And whoever will not receive you, when you go out of that city, shake off the very dust from your feet as a testimony against them."*

6 *So they departed and went through the towns, preaching the gospel and healing everywhere.*

7 *Now Herod the tetrarch heard of all that was done by Him; and he was perplexed, because it was said by some that John had risen from the dead,*

8 *and by some that Elijah had appeared, and by others that one of the old prophets had risen again.*

9 *Herod said, "John I have beheaded, but who is this of whom I hear such things?" So he sought to see Him.*

10 *And the apostles, when they had returned, told Him all that they had done. Then He took them and went aside privately into a deserted place belonging to the city called Bethsaida.*

Bethsaida (v. 10)—This city was on the north shore of Galilee, where the Jordan River enters the lake. Peter, Philip, and Andrew had all grown up there (John 1:44).

11 *But when the multitudes knew it, they followed Him; and He received them and spoke to them about the kingdom of God, and healed those who had need of healing.*

12 *When the day began to wear away, the twelve came and said to Him, "Send the multitude away, that they may go into the surrounding towns and country, and lodge and get provisions; for we are in a deserted place here."*

13 *But He said to them, "You give them something to eat." And they said, "We have no more than five*

about five thousand men (v. 14)—Counting women and children, the actual size of the crowd may have been closer to 20,000.

loaves and two fish, unless we go and buy food for all these people."

14 For there were about five thousand men. Then He said to His disciples, "Make them sit down in groups of fifty."

15 And they did so, and made them all sit down.

16 Then He took the five loaves and the two fish, and looking up to heaven, He blessed and broke them, and gave them to the disciples to set before the multitude.

17 So they all ate and were filled, and twelve baskets of the leftover fragments were taken up by them.

18 And it happened, as He was alone praying, that His disciples joined Him, and He asked them, saying, "Who do the crowds say that I am?"

19 So they answered and said, "John the Baptist, but some say Elijah; and others say that one of the old prophets has risen again."

20 He said to them, "But who do you say that I am?" Peter answered and said, "The Christ of God."

21 And He strictly warned and commanded them to tell this to no one,

22 saying, "The Son of Man must suffer many things, and be rejected by the elders and chief priests and scribes, and be killed, and be raised the third day."

23 Then He said to them all, "If anyone desires to come after Me, let him deny himself, and take up his cross daily, and follow Me.

whoever loses his life for My sake (v. 24)—Aside from the command "follow Me," this saying is repeated more times in the Gospels than any other saying of Christ (17:33; Matt. 10:39; 16:25; Mark 8:35; John 12:25).

24 For whoever desires to save his life will lose it, but whoever loses his life for My sake will save it.

25 For what profit is it to a man if he gains the whole world, and is himself destroyed or lost?

26 For whoever is ashamed of Me and My words, of him the Son of Man will be ashamed when He comes in His own glory, and in His Father's, and of the holy angels.

27 But I tell you truly, there are some standing here who shall not taste death till they see the kingdom of God."

28 Now it came to pass, about eight days after these sayings, that He took Peter, John, and James and went up on the mountain to pray.

29 As He prayed, the appearance of His face was altered, and His robe became white and glistening.

30 And behold, two men talked with Him, who were Moses and Elijah,

31 who appeared in glory and spoke of His decease which He was about to accomplish at Jerusalem.

32 But Peter and those with him were heavy with sleep; and when they were fully awake, they saw His glory and the two men who stood with Him.

33 Then it happened, as they were parting from Him, that Peter said to Jesus, "Master, it is good for us to be here; and let us make three tabernacles: one for You, one for Moses, and one for Elijah"—not knowing what he said.

34 While he was saying this, a cloud came and overshadowed them; and they were fearful as they entered the cloud.

35 And a voice came out of the cloud, saying, "This is My beloved Son. Hear Him!"

36 When the voice had ceased, Jesus was found alone. But they kept quiet, and told no one in those days any of the things they had seen.

37 Now it happened on the next day, when they had come down from the mountain, that a great multitude met Him.

38 Suddenly a man from the multitude cried out, saying, "Teacher, I implore You, look on my son, for he is my only child.

39 And behold, a spirit seizes him, and he suddenly cries out; it convulses him so that he foams at the mouth; and it departs from him with great difficulty, bruising him.

40 So I implored Your disciples to cast it out, but they could not."

41 Then Jesus answered and said, "O faithless and perverse generation, how long shall I be with you and bear with you? Bring your son here."

after these sayings (v. 28)— This expression ties the promise of seeing the kingdom (v. 27) to the events that follow.

glistening (v. 31)—Literally "emitting light," this word is used only here in the New Testament; it suggests a brilliant flashing light, similar to lightning.

a spirit seizes him (v. 39)—no mere case of epilepsy; plainly demon possession

42 *And as he was still coming, the demon threw him down and convulsed him. Then Jesus rebuked the unclean spirit, healed the child, and gave him back to his father.*

43 *And they were all amazed at the majesty of God. But while everyone marveled at all the things which Jesus did, He said to His disciples,*

44 *"Let these words sink down into your ears, for the Son of Man is about to be betrayed into the hands of men."*

45 *But they did not understand this saying, and it was hidden from them so that they did not perceive it; and they were afraid to ask Him about this saying.*

46 *Then a dispute arose among them as to which of them would be greatest.*

47 *And Jesus, perceiving the thought of their heart, took a little child and set him by Him,*

48 *and said to them, "Whoever receives this little child in My name receives Me; and whoever receives Me receives Him who sent Me. For he who is least among you all will be great."*

49 *Now John answered and said, "Master, we saw someone casting out demons in Your name, and we forbade him because he does not follow with us."*

50 *But Jesus said to him, "Do not forbid him, for he who is not against us is on our side."*

he who is least . . . will be great (v. 48)—The only way to pre-eminence in Christ's kingdom is by sacrifice and self-denial.

1) Luke 6:17–38 features Christ's teaching. List at least five kingdom truths or principles from these verses.

_____

_____

_____

2) What is the message of the parable of the two foundations (6:46–49)?

_____

_____

_____

3) Luke 7:17–30 contains an interesting conversation between Christ and the disciples of John the Baptist. What prompted John to ask, "Are You the Coming One?"

_____

_____

_____

_____

4) What is the message in Christ's parable of the lamp (Luke 8:16–18)? What is the meaning of verse 18?

_____

_____

_____

_____

5) How does Jesus define or describe the true cost of discipleship in 9:23–26?

_____

_____

_____

_____

GOING DEEPER

In Luke 9, Jesus fed five thousand people. Read Mark 6:35–44 for another account of the same miracle.

35 *When the day was now far spent, His disciples came to Him and said, "This is a deserted place, and already the hour is late.*

36 *Send them away, that they may go into the surrounding country and villages and buy themselves bread; for they have nothing to eat."*

37 *But He answered and said to them, "You give them something to eat." And they said to Him, "Shall we go and buy two hundred denarii worth of bread and give them something to eat?"*

38 *But He said to them, "How many loaves do you have? Go and see." And when they found out they said, "Five, and two fish."*

39 *Then He commanded them to make them all sit down in groups on the green grass.*

40 *So they sat down in ranks, in hundreds and in fifties.*

41 *And when He had taken the five loaves and the two fish, He looked up to heaven, blessed and broke the loaves, and gave them to His disciples to set before them; and the two fish He divided among them all.*

42 *So they all ate and were filled.*

43 *And they took up twelve baskets full of fragments and of the fish.*

44 *Now those who had eaten the loaves were about five thousand men.*

EXPLORING THE MEANING

6) What additional details does Mark reveal about this miracle—the only miracle other than the Resurrection that appears in all four Gospels?

_____

_____

_____

7) Some people attack the Christian faith, labeling it sexist and demeaning to women. How does Luke 8:1–3 (and Christ's overall treatment of women) serve to refute these charges?

_____

_____

8) What does the Transfiguration (9:27–36) reveal about Christ? What is the meaning of Peter's words?

_____

_____

9) What do Jesus' words in 9:49–50 suggest about the idea of being spiritually "neutral"? Is it possible to be mildly or moderately committed to Christ? Why or why not?

_____

_____

_____

Truth for Today

A disciple is someone who confesses Christ as Lord and Savior, believes that God has raised Him from the dead, and declares this belief publicly through baptism. He is not some sort of "upper–level" Christian. You don't have to wait to become a disciple at some future time in your Christian life when you have reached a certain level of maturity. According to Matthew 28:19–20, a disciple is made at the moment of salvation. Some claim that there are many Christians who are not disciples. But you cannot separate discipleship from conversion. When someone is saved, he or she receives a submissive spirit that manifests itself by a willingness to make a public confession and obey whatever else Christ commands.

Reflecting on the Text

10) Based on the definition given above, are you a disciple?

_____

_____

_____

_____

_____

11) In this study you have examined many of the words and works of Christ. What has impacted you most deeply? What new insight have you received about the Person of Jesus Christ?

_____

_____

_____

12) James 1:22 is the familiar verse that admonishes us to be "doers of the Word." What specifically are you going to do today with the truth you've just been exposed to?

_____

_____

_____

PERSONAL RESPONSE

Write out additional reflections, questions you may have, or a prayer.

~5~
CHRIST'S AUDIENCE

DRAWING NEAR

Who would you say is the most devoted Christian you know? Describe this individual. What practices or spiritual disciplines does he/she faithfully engage in?

_____

_____

_____

_____

_____

Think back over your own spiritual experience. When would you say you were most zealous for God? Why?

_____

_____

_____

_____

THE CONTEXT

Following his time in Galilee, Jesus began looking toward Jerusalem. Luke's narrative becomes a travelogue of that long journey to the cross. This was a dramatic turning point in Christ's ministry. From this point forward, Galilee was no longer His base of operation. We know from a comparison of the Gospels that during this period of Christ's ministry, He made short visits to Jerusalem to celebrate feasts. Nonetheless, those brief visits were only interludes in this period of ministry that would culminate in a final journey to Jerusalem. Luke dramatically underscored this turning point by showing Christ's determination to complete His mission of going to the cross. Luke 10 includes the sending out of the seventy, and the beloved parable of the Good Samaritan. It concludes with the delightful account of Jesus visiting in the home of Mary, Martha, and their brother Lazarus.

Keys to the Text

The Spirit: This comes from the Greek word *pneuma*, meaning "to breathe" or "to blow." It is sometimes used to refer to the wind and sometimes to life itself (see John 3:8). It can refer to the life of angels, demons, and human beings. Yet this word is also used for the Spirit of God (see Luke 10:21), that is, the Holy Spirit, the third Person of the Trinity, the One who lives inside believers. This same Spirit is called "the Spirit of Jesus Christ" (Phil. 1:19). This title emphasizes the unity of action between Jesus and the Spirit that permeates the gospel of Luke and the Acts of the Apostles. During the days of Jesus' earthly ministry, the disciples were directed by Jesus Himself. After His resurrection and ascension, they were led by the Spirit of Jesus.

Unleashing the Text

Read 9:51–10:42, noting the key words and definitions next to the passage.

Luke 9:51–10:42 (NKJV)

51 *Now it came to pass, when the time had come for Him to be received up, that He steadfastly set His face to go to Jerusalem,*

Samaritans (v. 52)—descendants of Jewish mixed marriages from the days of captivity; they had devised their own worship, a hybrid of Judaism and paganism, with a temple of their own on Mount Gerizim; considered unclean by the Jews

52 *and sent messengers before His face. And as they went, they entered a village of the Samaritans, to prepare for Him.*

53 *But they did not receive Him, because His face was set for the journey to Jerusalem.*

James and John (v. 52)—Jesus nicknamed these two brothers "Boanerges"—Sons of Thunder (Mark 3:17)—a fitting title, apparently.

54 *And when His disciples James and John saw this, they said, "Lord, do You want us to command fire to come down from heaven and consume them, just as Elijah did?"*

rebuked them (v. 55)—The Samaritans were intolerant, and their worship was pagan at heart, yet the Lord would not retaliate with force against them.

55 *But He turned and rebuked them, and said, "You do not know what manner of spirit you are of.*

56 *For the Son of Man did not come to destroy men's lives but to save them." And they went to another village.*

57 *Now it happened as they journeyed on the road, that someone said to Him, "Lord, I will follow You wherever You go."*

58 *And Jesus said to him, "Foxes have holes and birds of the air have nests, but the Son of Man has nowhere to lay His head."*

59 *Then He said to another, "Follow Me." But he said,*
"Lord, let me first go and bury my father."

60 *Jesus said to him, "Let the dead bury their own*
dead, but you go and preach the kingdom of God."

61 *And another also said, "Lord, I will follow You, but*
let me first go and bid them farewell who are at my
house."

62 *But Jesus said to him, "No one, having put his hand*
to the plow, and looking back, is fit for the kingdom
of God."

10:1 *After these things the Lord appointed seventy*
others also, and sent them two by two before His
face into every city and place where He Himself was
about to go.

2 *Then He said to them, "The harvest truly is great,*
but the laborers are few; therefore pray the Lord of
the harvest to send out laborers into His harvest.

3 *Go your way; behold, I send you out as lambs*
among wolves.

4 *Carry neither money bag, knapsack, nor sandals;*
and greet no one along the road.

5 *But whatever house you enter, first say, 'Peace to*
this house.'

6 *And if a son of peace is there, your peace will rest on*
it; if not, it will return to you.

7 *And remain in the same house, eating and drinking*
such things as they give, for the laborer is worthy of
his wages. Do not go from house to house.

8 *Whatever city you enter, and they receive you, eat*
such things as are set before you.

9 *And heal the sick there, and say to them, 'The*
kingdom of God has come near to you.'

10 *But whatever city you enter, and they do not receive*
you, go out into its streets and say,

11 *'The very dust of your city which clings to us we*
wipe off against you. Nevertheless know this, that
the kingdom of God has come near you.'

12 *But I say to you that it will be more tolerable in that*
Day for Sodom than for that city.

looking back (v. 62)—A plow-man looking back cuts a crooked furrow.

two by two (10:1)—as the Twelve had been sent (Mark 6:7)

lambs among wolves (v. 3)—Jesus warns that they will face hostility and spiritual danger.

greet no one (v. 4)—A greeting in that culture was an elaborate ceremony, involving many formalities, perhaps even a meal, and long delays; everything in Jesus' instructions speak of the shortness of time and the great urgency of the task.

returned with joy (v. 17)—How long the mission lasted is not recorded; perhaps several weeks.

I saw Satan fall. (v. 18)—In this context, it appears Jesus' meaning was, "Don't be so surprised that the demons are subject to you; I saw their commander cast out of heaven, so it is no wonder if his minions are cast out on earth."

do not rejoice in this (v. 20)—Rather than being so enthralled with extraordinary manifestations, such as power over demons and the ability to work miracles, they should have realized that the greatest wonder of all is the reality of salvation.

lawyer (v. 25)—i.e., a scribe who was supposedly an expert in the law of God

13 *"Woe to you, Chorazin! Woe to you, Bethsaida! For if the mighty works which were done in you had been done in Tyre and Sidon, they would have repented long ago, sitting in sackcloth and ashes.*

14 *But it will be more tolerable for Tyre and Sidon at the judgment than for you.*

15 *And you, Capernaum, who are exalted to heaven, will be brought down to Hades.*

16 *He who hears you hears Me, he who rejects you rejects Me, and he who rejects Me rejects Him who sent Me."*

17 *Then the seventy returned with joy, saying, "Lord, even the demons are subject to us in Your name."*

18 *And He said to them, "I saw Satan fall like lightning from heaven.*

19 *Behold, I give you the authority to trample on serpents and scorpions, and over all the power of the enemy, and nothing shall by any means hurt you.*

20 *Nevertheless do not rejoice in this, that the spirits are subject to you, but rather rejoice because your names are written in heaven."*

21 *In that hour Jesus rejoiced in the Spirit and said, "I thank You, Father, Lord of heaven and earth, that You have hidden these things from the wise and prudent and revealed them to babes. Even so, Father, for so it seemed good in Your sight.*

22 *All things have been delivered to Me by My Father, and no one knows who the Son is except the Father, and who the Father is except the Son, and the one to whom the Son wills to reveal Him."*

23 *Then He turned to His disciples and said privately, "Blessed are the eyes which see the things you see;*

24 *for I tell you that many prophets and kings have desired to see what you see, and have not seen it, and to hear what you hear, and have not heard it."*

25 *And behold, a certain lawyer stood up and tested Him, saying, "Teacher, what shall I do to inherit eternal life?"*

26 He said to him, "What is written in the law? What is your reading of it?"

27 So he answered and said, "'You shall love the LORD your God with all your heart, with all your soul, with all your strength, and with all your mind,' and 'your neighbor as yourself.'"

28 And He said to him, "You have answered rightly; do this and you will live."

29 But he, wanting to justify himself, said to Jesus, "And who is my neighbor?"

30 Then Jesus answered and said: "A certain man went down from Jerusalem to Jericho, and fell among thieves, who stripped him of his clothing, wounded him, and departed, leaving him half dead.

31 Now by chance a certain priest came down that road. And when he saw him, he passed by on the other side.

32 Likewise a Levite, when he arrived at the place, came and looked, and passed by on the other side.

33 But a certain Samaritan, as he journeyed, came where he was. And when he saw him, he had compassion.

34 So he went to him and bandaged his wounds, pouring on oil and wine; and he set him on his own animal, brought him to an inn, and took care of him.

35 On the next day, when he departed, he took out two denarii, gave them to the innkeeper, and said to him, 'Take care of him; and whatever more you spend, when I come again, I will repay you.'

36 So which of these three do you think was neighbor to him who fell among the thieves?"

37 And he said, "He who showed mercy on him." Then Jesus said to him, "Go and do likewise."

38 Now it happened as they went that He entered a certain village; and a certain woman named Martha welcomed Him into her house.

39 And she had a sister called Mary, who also sat at Jesus' feet and heard His word.

do this and you will live (v. 28)—See Exodus 20:11; Leviticus 18:5; and Ezekiel 20:11. "Do and live" is the promise of the Law. But since no sinner can obey perfectly, the impossible demands of the Law are meant to drive us to seek divine mercy (Gal. 3:10–13, 22–25). This man should have responded with a confession of his own guilt, rather than self-justification (v. 29).

down from Jerusalem to Jericho (v. 30)—Notorious for being beset with thieves and danger, that stretch of road was a rocky, winding, treacherous descent of about 3,300 feet in 17 miles.

oil and wine (v. 34)—Carried by travelers in small amounts as a kind of first-aid kit, the wine was antiseptic, and the oil soothing and healing.

neighbor to him (v. 36)—Jesus reversed the lawyer's original question (v. 29). The lawyer assumed it was up to others to prove themselves neighbor to him; Jesus' reply makes it clear that each has a responsibility to be a neighbor—especially to those who are in need.

a certain village (v. 38)—Bethany, two miles east of the temple in Jerusalem, on the eastern slope of the Mount of Olives; the home of Mary, Martha, and Lazarus (see John 11:1)

distracted (v. 40)—Literally "dragging all around," Martha was in a tumult, fussing with details that were unnecessarily elaborate.

one thing . . . good part (v. 42)—The one thing necessary was exemplified by Mary—an attitude of worship and meditation, listening with an open mind and heart to Jesus' words.

40 But Martha was distracted with much serving, and she approached Him and said, "Lord, do You not care that my sister has left me to serve alone? Therefore tell her to help me."

41 And Jesus answered and said to her, "Martha, Martha, you are worried and troubled about many things.

42 But one thing is needed, and Mary has chosen that good part, which will not be taken away from her."

1) What did the interesting request made by James and John reveal about them (9:54)?

_____

_____

_____

_____

2) Three "would-be" followers of Jesus approached Him in Luke 9:57–62. Describe each of these brief conversations.

_____

_____

_____

_____

3) In Luke 10:1–24, we find an account of an evangelistic mission involving seventy other disciples of Jesus. What was the result of this ministry effort?

_____

_____

_____

_____

4) How did Jesus answer when a lawyer asked him, "What shall I do to inherit eternal life?" (10:25–37)? Does this answer surprise you, and why?

_____

_____

_____

_____

5) How did Jesus respond to the differences in Mary and Martha (10:38–42)?

_____

_____

_____

_____

Going Deeper

Jesus reminded Martha that time with Him was the "good part." For more about dwelling in Christ, read John 15:1–11.

1 *"I am the true vine, and My Father is the vinedresser.*
2 *Every branch in Me that does not bear fruit He takes away; and every branch that bears fruit He prunes, that it may bear more fruit.*
3 *You are already clean because of the word which I have spoken to you.*
4 *Abide in Me, and I in you. As the branch cannot bear fruit of itself, unless it abides in the vine, neither can you, unless you abide in Me.*
5 *"I am the vine, you are the branches. He who abides in Me, and I in him, bears much fruit; for without Me you can do nothing.*
6 *If anyone does not abide in Me, he is cast out as a branch and is withered; and they gather them and throw them into the fire, and they are burned.*
7 *If you abide in Me, and My words abide in you, you will ask what you desire, and it shall be done for you.*
8 *By this My Father is glorified, that you bear much fruit; so you will be My disciples.*
9 *"As the Father loved Me, I also have loved you; abide in My love.*
10 *If you keep My commandments, you will abide in My love, just as I have kept My Father's commandments and abide in His love.*
11 *"These things I have spoken to you, that My joy may remain in you, and that your joy may be full."*

Exploring the Meaning

6) Ponder Jesus' words here about "abiding in Him" in light of His conversation with Martha (Luke 10:38–42). What is the "big idea" in these two passages? Why is it sometimes easier for Christians to "do things" for Christ rather than to spend time being with Christ?

_____

_____

_____

_____

7) What do you think is behind the anger and indignation of James and John in Luke 9:54? What would prompt such a retaliatory response?

_____

_____

_____

_____

8) What did Jesus mean in Luke 10:19–20? What does it mean that someone's name is "written in heaven"?

_____

_____

_____

_____

9) When Jesus confronted Martha about her attitude in Luke 10:41–42, was He condemning her efficient, hardworking desire to serve and be productive? How do you know?

_____

_____

_____

_____

Truth for Today

You can pay nothing to earn salvation; yet living for Christ is a serious matter of discipleship. To be a Christian means to rely on Christ's power rather than your own and to be willing to forsake your way for His. Being a Christian can mean facing persecution, ridicule, and tribulation. Jesus forewarned the disciples, "If they persecuted Me, they will also persecute you" (John 15:20 NKJV). But with His warning about the cost of discipleship, the Lord promised that your heart would rejoice "and your joy no one will take from you" (John 16:22 NKJV). And He also told His followers to "be of good cheer, I have overcome the world" (John 16:33 NKJV). You won't escape the difficulties of discipleship, but Jesus will enable you to handle them.

Reflecting on the Text

10) What has been the most difficult experience you've had to endure since you became a follower of Christ?

_____

_____

_____

11) All of Luke's gospel, and certainly the passage you've studied in this lesson, indicates that Christ desires His followers to be engaged in kingdom ministry. What needs to change—either attitudes or actions—with regard to your own ministry involvement?

_____

_____

_____

12) How specifically can you avoid the "Martha syndrome" today? What is your plan for ceasing all activity just to be in Christ's presence—adoring and enjoying Him?

_____

_____

_____

PERSONAL RESPONSE

Write out additional reflections, questions you may have, or a prayer.

～6～
CHRIST'S ETERNAL REMINDERS

Luke 11:1–13:35

DRAWING NEAR

What five words would you use to describe your prayer life?

_____

_____

_____

Do you have a special time and place set aside for conversing with God—a daily appointment with Him? Why or why not?

_____

_____

_____

THE CONTEXT

Having concluded His Galilean ministry, the Son of Man's destination is now Jerusalem, where He will die for the sins of the world. Here is a record of Jesus' brief ministry in Bethany and Judea. Chapter 11 begins with Christ's teaching on prayer, then moves into a warning about the impossibility of spiritual neutrality. The chapter concludes with a pronouncement of woes on the hardhearted and hardheaded Pharisees and teachers of the Law, who have refused Christ's kingship. In light of this rejection, Christ issues some stern warnings, mixed with parables. He denounces hypocrisy, covetousness, and the foolish refusal of so many to "discern this time." In between, Christ counsels His followers to fear God and to resist the urge to worry or be fearful.

KEYS TO THE TEXT

Repent: Jesus' message was a message of repentance, for the kingdom of God was near. To repent means to turn from sin, to change one's orientation, to turn around and seek a new way. _Metanoia_, the Greek word, literally means "a change of perception," a change in the way we see something. To repent, therefore, is to change the way a person looks at sin and the way he looks at righteousness. It involves a change of opinion, of direction, of life itself. To repent is to have a

73

radical change of heart and will—and, consequently, of behavior. Repentance was and is the first demand of the gospel, the first requirement of salvation, and the first element of the saving work of the Spirit in the soul.

Jewish Religious Leaders: This group was made up of Pharisees, Sadducees, scribes, and teachers of the Law. They were threatened by Jesus' popularity and eventually sought to kill him. The *Pharisees* were a small legalistic sect of the Jews known for their rigid adherence to the ceremonial fine points of the Law. Jesus rebuked them for using human tradition to nullify Scripture and for rank hypocrisy. *Scribes* were primarily Pharisees and authorities on Jewish law. Sometimes they are referred to as "lawyers." The *Sadducees* denied the resurrection of the dead and the existence of angels and accepted only the Pentateuch as authoritative. In the days of Herod, their sect controlled the temple.

UNLEASHING THE TEXT

Read 11:1–13:35, noting the key words and definitions next to the passage.

Luke 11:1–13:35 (NKJV)

Lord, teach us to pray (v. 1)—Rabbis often composed prayers for their disciples to recite.

1 Now it came to pass, as He was praying in a certain place, when He ceased, that one of His disciples said to Him, "Lord, teach us to pray, as John also taught his disciples."

Your name (v. 2)—God's name represents all His character and attributes.

2 So He said to them, "When you pray, say: Our Father in heaven, hallowed be Your name. Your kingdom come. Your will be done on earth as it is in heaven.

3 Give us day by day our daily bread.

4 And forgive us our sins, for we also forgive everyone who is indebted to us. And do not lead us into temptation, but deliver us from the evil one."

5 And He said to them, "Which of you shall have a friend, and go to him at midnight and say to him, 'Friend, lend me three loaves;

6 for a friend of mine has come to me on his journey, and I have nothing to set before him';

7 and he will answer from within and say, 'Do not trouble me; the door is now shut, and my children are with me in bed; I cannot rise and give to you'?

8 *I say to you, though he will not rise and give to him because he is his friend, yet because of his persistence he will rise and give him as many as he needs.*

9 *"So I say to you, ask, and it will be given to you; seek, and you will find; knock, and it will be opened to you.*

10 *For everyone who asks receives, and he who seeks finds, and to him who knocks it will be opened.*

11 *If a son asks for bread from any father among you, will he give him a stone? Or if he asks for a fish, will he give him a serpent instead of a fish?*

12 *Or if he asks for an egg, will he offer him a scorpion?*

13 *If you then, being evil, know how to give good gifts to your children, how much more will your heavenly Father give the Holy Spirit to those who ask Him!"*

14 *And He was casting out a demon, and it was mute. So it was, when the demon had gone out, that the mute spoke; and the multitudes marveled.*

15 *But some of them said, "He casts out demons by Beelzebub, the ruler of the demons."*

16 *Others, testing Him, sought from Him a sign from heaven.*

17 *But He, knowing their thoughts, said to them: "Every kingdom divided against itself is brought to desolation, and a house divided against a house falls.*

18 *If Satan also is divided against himself, how will his kingdom stand? Because you say I cast out demons by Beelzebub.*

19 *And if I cast out demons by Beelzebub, by whom do your sons cast them out? Therefore they will be your judges.*

20 *But if I cast out demons with the finger of God, surely the kingdom of God has come upon you.*

21 *When a strong man, fully armed, guards his own palace, his goods are in peace.*

22 *But when a stronger than he comes upon him and overcomes him, he takes from him all his armor in which he trusted, and divides his spoils.*

persistence (v. 8)—The word can even mean "impudence." It conveys the ideas of urgency, audacity, earnestness, boldness, and relentlessness—like the persistent asking of a desperate beggar.

being evil (v. 13)—i.e., by nature

Beelzebub (v. 15)—Originally this referred to Baal-Zebul ("Baal, the prince"), chief god of the Philistine city of Ekron; the Israelites disdainfully referred to him as Baal-Zebub ("Lord of Flies").

a sign from heaven (v. 16)—i.e., a miraculous work of cosmological proportions, like the rearranging of the constellations, or something far greater than the casting out of a demon, which they had just witnessed

by whom do your sons cast them out? (v. 19)—There were Jewish exorcists who claimed power to cast out demons (Acts 19:13–15). Jesus' point was that if such exorcisms could be done via satanic power, the Pharisaical exorcists must be suspect as well.

unclean spirit goes out (v. 24)—Christ was characterizing the work of the phony Jewish exorcists; what appears to be a true exorcism is merely a temporary respite, after which the demon returns with seven others (v. 26).

It seeks a sign (v. 29)—Jesus always declined to give signs on demand; evidences were not the means by which He appealed to unbelievers.

The lamp of the body (v. 34)—Here the eye is the "lamp"—i.e., the source of light—for the body; the problem with the Pharisees was their perception, not a lack of light. They did not need a sign; they needed hearts to believe the great display of divine power they had already seen.

23 *He who is not with Me is against Me, and he who does not gather with Me scatters.*

24 *"When an unclean spirit goes out of a man, he goes through dry places, seeking rest; and finding none, he says, 'I will return to my house from which I came.'*

25 *And when he comes, he finds it swept and put in order.*

26 *Then he goes and takes with him seven other spirits more wicked than himself, and they enter and dwell there; and the last state of that man is worse than the first."*

27 *And it happened, as He spoke these things, that a certain woman from the crowd raised her voice and said to Him, "Blessed is the womb that bore You, and the breasts which nursed You!"*

28 *But He said, "More than that, blessed are those who hear the word of God and keep it!"*

29 *And while the crowds were thickly gathered together, He began to say, "This is an evil generation. It seeks a sign, and no sign will be given to it except the sign of Jonah the prophet.*

30 *For as Jonah became a sign to the Ninevites, so also the Son of Man will be to this generation.*

31 *The queen of the South will rise up in the judgment with the men of this generation and condemn them, for she came from the ends of the earth to hear the wisdom of Solomon; and indeed a greater than Solomon is here.*

32 *The men of Nineveh will rise up in the judgment with this generation and condemn it, for they repented at the preaching of Jonah; and indeed a greater than Jonah is here.*

33 *"No one, when he has lit a lamp, puts it in a secret place or under a basket, but on a lampstand, that those who come in may see the light.*

34 *The lamp of the body is the eye. Therefore, when your eye is good, your whole body also is full of light. But when your eye is bad, your body also is full of darkness.*

35 *Therefore take heed that the light which is in you is not darkness.*

36 *If then your whole body is full of light, having no part dark, the whole body will be full of light, as when the bright shining of a lamp gives you light."*

37 *And as He spoke, a certain Pharisee asked Him to dine with him. So He went in and sat down to eat.*

38 *When the Pharisee saw it, he marveled that He had not first washed before dinner.*

He had not first washed (v. 38)—a concern with ceremony, not hygiene

39 *Then the Lord said to him, "Now you Pharisees make the outside of the cup and dish clean, but your inward part is full of greed and wickedness.*

40 *Foolish ones! Did not He who made the outside make the inside also?*

Foolish ones! (v. 40)—This refers to individuals who lack understanding. This was the truth and not the sort of coarse name-calling Christ forbade in Matthew 5:22.

41 *But rather give alms of such things as you have; then indeed all things are clean to you.*

42 *"But woe to you Pharisees! For you tithe mint and rue and all manner of herbs, and pass by justice and the love of God. These you ought to have done, without leaving the others undone.*

43 *Woe to you Pharisees! For you love the best seats in the synagogues and greetings in the marketplaces.*

44 *Woe to you, scribes and Pharisees, hypocrites! For you are like graves which are not seen, and the men who walk over them are not aware of them."*

graves which are not seen (v. 44)— hidden sources of defilement which were carefully concealed

45 *Then one of the lawyers answered and said to Him, "Teacher, by saying these things You reproach us also."*

46 *And He said, "Woe to you also, lawyers! For you load men with burdens hard to bear, and you yourselves do not touch the burdens with one of your fingers.*

47 *Woe to you! For you build the tombs of the prophets, and your fathers killed them.*

48 *In fact, you bear witness that you approve the deeds of your fathers; for they indeed killed them, and you build their tombs.*

49 *Therefore the wisdom of God also said, 'I will send them prophets and apostles, and some of them they will kill and persecute,'*

50 *that the blood of all the prophets which was shed*
   from the foundation of the world may be required of
   this generation,

51 *from the blood of Abel to the blood of Zechariah*
   who perished between the altar and the temple. Yes,
   I say to you, it shall be required of this generation.

52 *"Woe to you lawyers! For you have taken away the*
   key of knowledge. You did not enter in yourselves,
   and those who were entering in you hindered."

53 *And as He said these things to them, the scribes and*
   the Pharisees began to assail Him vehemently, and
   to cross-examine Him about many things,

54 *lying in wait for Him, and seeking to catch Him in*
   something He might say, that they might accuse
   Him.

12:1 *In the meantime, when an innumerable multitude*
   of people had gathered together, so that they
   trampled one another, He began to say to His
   disciples first of all, "Beware of the leaven of the
   Pharisees, which is hypocrisy.

2 *For there is nothing covered that will not be*
   revealed, nor hidden that will not be known.

3 *Therefore whatever you have spoken in the dark will*
   be heard in the light, and what you have spoken in
   the ear in inner rooms will be proclaimed on the
   housetops.

4 *"And I say to you, My friends, do not be afraid of*
   those who kill the body, and after that have no more
   that they can do.

5 *But I will show you whom you should fear: Fear*
   Him who, after He has killed, has power to cast into
   hell; yes, I say to you, fear Him!

6 *"Are not five sparrows sold for two copper coins?*
   And not one of them is forgotten before God.

7 *But the very hairs of your head are all numbered.*
   Do not fear therefore; you are of more value than
   many sparrows.

8 *"Also I say to you, whoever confesses Me before men,*
   him the Son of Man also will confess before the
   angels of God.

the key of knowledge (v. 52)—
They had locked up the truth of
the Scriptures and thrown away
the key by imposing their faulty
interpretations and human traditions on God's Word.

**not one of them is forgotten
before God** (12:6)—Divine
providence governs even the
most inconsequential details of
God's creation.

9 But he who denies Me before men will be denied before the angels of God.

10 "And anyone who speaks a word against the Son of Man, it will be forgiven him; but to him who blasphemes against the Holy Spirit, it will not be forgiven.

11 "Now when they bring you to the synagogues and magistrates and authorities, do not worry about how or what you should answer, or what you should say.

12 For the Holy Spirit will teach you in that very hour what you ought to say."

13 Then one from the crowd said to Him, "Teacher, tell my brother to divide the inheritance with me."

14 But He said to him, "Man, who made Me a judge or an arbitrator over you?"

15 And He said to them, "Take heed and beware of covetousness, for one's life does not consist in the abundance of the things he possesses."

16 Then He spoke a parable to them, saying: "The ground of a certain rich man yielded plentifully.

17 And he thought within himself, saying, 'What shall I do, since I have no room to store my crops?'

18 So he said, 'I will do this: I will pull down my barns and build greater, and there I will store all my crops and my goods.

19 And I will say to my soul, "Soul, you have many goods laid up for many years; take your ease; eat, drink, and be merry." '

20 But God said to him, 'Fool! This night your soul will be required of you; then whose will those things be which you have provided?'

21 "So is he who lays up treasure for himself, and is not rich toward God."

22 Then He said to His disciples, "Therefore I say to you, do not worry about your life, what you will eat; nor about the body, what you will put on.

23 Life is more than food, and the body is more than clothing.

he who denies Me before men (v. 9)—This describes a soul-damning denial of Christ—not the sort of temporary wavering Peter was guilty of (22:56–62), but the sin of those who, through fear, shame, neglect, delay, or love of the world, reject all evidence and revelation and decline to confess Christ as Savior and King until it is too late.

blasphemes against the Holy Spirit (v. 10)—not a sin of ignorance, but a deliberate, willful, settled hostility toward Christ—exemplified by the Pharisees, when in Matthew 12 they attributed to Satan the work of Christ

who made Me a judge? (v. 14)—One of Christ's roles is that of Judge of all the earth (John 5:22), but He did not come to be an arbiter of petty earthly disputes.

24 Consider the ravens, for they neither sow nor reap, which have neither storehouse nor barn; and God feeds them. Of how much more value are you than the birds?

25 And which of you by worrying can add one cubit to his stature?

26 If you then are not able to do the least, why are you anxious for the rest?

27 Consider the lilies, how they grow: they neither toil nor spin; and yet I say to you, even Solomon in all his glory was not arrayed like one of these.

28 If then God so clothes the grass, which today is in the field and tomorrow is thrown into the oven, how much more will He clothe you, O you of little faith?

29 "And do not seek what you should eat or what you should drink, nor have an anxious mind.

30 For all these things the nations of the world seek after, and your Father knows that you need these things.

31 But seek the kingdom of God, and all these things shall be added to you.

32 "Do not fear, little flock, for it is your Father's good pleasure to give you the kingdom.

33 Sell what you have and give alms; provide yourselves money bags which do not grow old, a treasure in the heavens that does not fail, where no thief approaches nor moth destroys.

34 For where your treasure is, there your heart will be also.

35 "Let your waist be girded and your lamps burning;

36 and you yourselves be like men who wait for their master, when he will return from the wedding, that when he comes and knocks they may open to him immediately.

37 Blessed are those servants whom the master, when he comes, will find watching. Assuredly, I say to you that he will gird himself and have them sit down to eat, and will come and serve them.

Sell what you have and give alms (v. 33)—Those who amassed earthly possessions, falsely thinking their security lay in material resources (vv. 16–20), needed to lay up treasure in heaven instead.

your heart will be also (v. 34)—Where one puts his money reveals the priorities of his heart.

watching (v. 37)—The key here is readiness at all times for Christ's return.

38 *And if he should come in the second watch, or come in the third watch, and find them so, blessed are those servants.*

39 *But know this, that if the master of the house had known what hour the thief would come, he would have watched and not allowed his house to be broken into.*

40 *Therefore you also be ready, for the Son of Man is coming at an hour you do not expect."*

41 *Then Peter said to Him, "Lord, do You speak this parable only to us, or to all people?"*

42 *And the Lord said, "Who then is that faithful and wise steward, whom his master will make ruler over his household, to give them their portion of food in due season?*

43 *Blessed is that servant whom his master will find so doing when he comes.*

44 *Truly, I say to you that he will make him ruler over all that he has.*

45 *But if that servant says in his heart, 'My master is delaying his coming,' and begins to beat the male and female servants, and to eat and drink and be drunk,*

46 *the master of that servant will come on a day when he is not looking for him, and at an hour when he is not aware, and will cut him in two and appoint him his portion with the unbelievers.*

47 *And that servant who knew his master's will, and did not prepare himself or do according to his will, shall be beaten with many stripes.*

48 *But he who did not know, yet committed things deserving of stripes, shall be beaten with few. For everyone to whom much is given, from him much will be required; and to whom much has been committed, of him they will ask the more.*

49 *"I came to send fire on the earth, and how I wish it were already kindled!*

50 *But I have a baptism to be baptized with, and how distressed I am till it is accomplished!*

Blessed is that servant (v. 43)—The faithful steward pictures the genuine believer, who manages well the spiritual riches God has put in his care for the benefit of others and receives honor and reward (v. 44).

cut him in two (v. 46)—i.e., utterly destroy him; speaks of the severity of final judgment of unbelievers

a baptism (v. 50)—a baptism of suffering, referring to Christ's death

51 Do you suppose that I came to give peace on earth? I tell you, not at all, but rather division.

52 For from now on five in one house will be divided: three against two, and two against three.

53 Father will be divided against son and son against father, mother against daughter and daughter against mother, mother-in-law against her daughter-in-law and daughter-in-law against her mother-in-law."

54 Then He also said to the multitudes, "Whenever you see a cloud rising out of the west, immediately you say, 'A shower is coming'; and so it is.

55 And when you see the south wind blow, you say, 'There will be hot weather'; and there is.

56 Hypocrites! You can discern the face of the sky and of the earth, but how is it you do not discern this time?

57 "Yes, and why, even of yourselves, do you not judge what is right?

58 When you go with your adversary to the magistrate, make every effort along the way to settle with him, lest he drag you to the judge, the judge deliver you to the officer, and the officer throw you into prison.

59 I tell you, you shall not depart from there till you have paid the very last mite."

13:1 There were present at that season some who told Him about the Galileans whose blood Pilate had mingled with their sacrifices.

2 And Jesus answered and said to them, "Do you suppose that these Galileans were worse sinners than all other Galileans, because they suffered such things?

3 I tell you, no; but unless you repent you will all likewise perish.

4 Or those eighteen on whom the tower in Siloam fell and killed them, do you think that they were worse sinners than all other men who dwelt in Jerusalem?

5 I tell you, no; but unless you repent you will all likewise perish."

Galileans whose blood Pilate had mingled with their sacrifices (13:1)—Evidently, some worshipers from Galilee were condemned by Rome—perhaps because they were seditious zealots—and were sought out and killed in the temple by Roman authorities while in the process of offering a sacrifice.

Siloam (v. 4)—This was an area at the southern end of the lower city of Jerusalem, where there was a well-known pool. Evidently, one of the towers guarding the aqueduct collapsed, killing some people. The question in the minds of people regarded the connection between calamity and iniquity. Jesus responded by saying that such a calamity was not God's way to single out an especially evil group for death, but as a means of warning to all sinners.

6 *He also spoke this parable: "A certain man had a fig tree planted in his vineyard, and he came seeking fruit on it and found none.*

7 *Then he said to the keeper of his vineyard, 'Look, for three years I have come seeking fruit on this fig tree and find none. Cut it down; why does it use up the ground?'*

8 *But he answered and said to him, 'Sir, let it alone this year also, until I dig around it and fertilize it.*

9 *And if it bears fruit, well. But if not, after that you can cut it down.' "*

10 *Now He was teaching in one of the synagogues on the Sabbath.*

11 *And behold, there was a woman who had a spirit of infirmity eighteen years, and was bent over and could in no way raise herself up.*

12 *But when Jesus saw her, He called her to Him and said to her, "Woman, you are loosed from your infirmity."*

13 *And He laid His hands on her, and immediately she was made straight, and glorified God.*

14 *But the ruler of the synagogue answered with indignation, because Jesus had healed on the Sabbath; and he said to the crowd, "There are six days on which men ought to work; therefore come and be healed on them, and not on the Sabbath day."*

15 *The Lord then answered him and said, "Hypocrite! Does not each one of you on the Sabbath loose his ox or donkey from the stall, and lead it away to water it?*

16 *So ought not this woman, being a daughter of Abraham, whom Satan has bound—think of it—for eighteen years, be loosed from this bond on the Sabbath?"*

17 *And when He said these things, all His adversaries were put to shame; and all the multitude rejoiced for all the glorious things that were done by Him.*

18 *Then He said, "What is the kingdom of God like? And to what shall I compare it?*

had a spirit of infirmity (v. 11)—Christ did not have to confront and drive out a demon, but simply declared her loosed (v. 12), so her case appears somewhat different from other cases of demonic possession He often encountered.

ruler (v. 14)—an eminent layman whose responsibilities included conducting meetings, caring for the building, and supervising the teaching in the synagogue

whom Satan has bound (v. 16)—This woman had apparently been permitted to suffer, not because of any evil she had done, but so the glory of God might be manifest in her (see John 9:3).

19 *It is like a mustard seed, which a man took and put in his garden; and it grew and became a large tree, and the birds of the air nested in its branches."*

20 *And again He said, "To what shall I liken the kingdom of God?*

21 *It is like leaven, which a woman took and hid in three measures of meal till it was all leavened."*

22 *And He went through the cities and villages, teaching, and journeying toward Jerusalem.*

23 *Then one said to Him, "Lord, are there few who are saved?" And He said to them,*

24 *"Strive to enter through the narrow gate, for many, I say to you, will seek to enter and will not be able.*

25 *When once the Master of the house has risen up and shut the door, and you begin to stand outside and knock at the door, saying, 'Lord, Lord, open for us,' and He will answer and say to you, 'I do not know you, where you are from,'*

26 *then you will begin to say, 'We ate and drank in Your presence, and You taught in our streets.'*

27 *But He will say, 'I tell you I do not know you, where you are from. Depart from Me, all you workers of iniquity.'*

28 *There will be weeping and gnashing of teeth, when you see Abraham and Isaac and Jacob and all the prophets in the kingdom of God, and yourselves thrust out.*

29 *They will come from the east and the west, from the north and the south, and sit down in the kingdom of God.*

30 *And indeed there are last who will be first, and there are first who will be last."*

31 *On that very day some Pharisees came, saying to Him, "Get out and depart from here, for Herod wants to kill You."*

32 *And He said to them, "Go, tell that fox, 'Behold, I cast out demons and perform cures today and tomorrow, and the third day I shall be perfected.'*

33 *Nevertheless I must journey today, tomorrow, and*

*the day following; for it cannot be that a prophet
should perish outside of Jerusalem.*

34 *"O Jerusalem, Jerusalem, the one who kills the
prophets and stones those who are sent to her! How
often I wanted to gather your children together, as
a hen gathers her brood under her wings, but you
were not willing!*

35 *See! Your house is left to you desolate; and assuredly,
I say to you, you shall not see Me until the time
comes when you say, 'Blessed is He who comes in
the name of the LORD!' "*

O Jerusalem, Jerusalem (v. 34)—
There is great tenderness in
these words, as seen in the
imagery of a hen with chick-
ens. This outpouring of divine
compassion foreshadows His
weeping over the city as He approached it for the final time
(19:41). Clearly, these are deep
and sincere emotions.

1) What are the main points of the two parables of the persistent friend and
the good father (Luke 11:5–13)?

_____

_____

_____

_____

2) How did the Jewish religious leaders explain Christ's power to perform
miracles, and how did Jesus respond to them (11:15–28)?

_____

_____

_____

3) Jesus had harsh words for the scribes and Pharisees (see 11:37–54). What
were His primary criticisms?

_____

_____

_____

4) Summarize Jesus' warnings and words of comfort to His followers in
Luke 12:1–12.

_____

_____

_____

5) What aspect of repentance does Jesus teach here (13:5–9)?

_____

_____

_____

Going Deeper

For more on the topic of repentance, read 2 Peter 3:1–9.

1 *Beloved, I now write to you this second epistle (in both of which I stir up your pure minds by way of reminder),*

2 *that you may be mindful of the words which were spoken before by the holy prophets, and of the commandment of us, the apostles of the Lord and Savior,*

3 *knowing this first: that scoffers will come in the last days, walking according to their own lusts,*

4 *and saying, "Where is the promise of His coming? For since the fathers fell asleep, all things continue as they were from the beginning of creation."*

5 *For this they willfully forget: that by the word of God the heavens were of old, and the earth standing out of water and in the water,*

6 *by which the world that then existed perished, being flooded with water.*

7 *But the heavens and the earth which are now preserved by the same word, are reserved for fire until the day of judgment and perdition of ungodly men.*

8 *But, beloved, do not forget this one thing, that with the Lord one day is as a thousand years, and a thousand years as one day.*

9 *The Lord is not slack concerning His promise, as some count slackness, but is longsuffering toward us, not willing that any should perish but that all should come to repentance.*

Exploring the Meaning

6) Considering this passage along with Jesus' words in Luke 13:34–35, what do you learn about the heart of God? About the heart of some people?

_____

_____

_____

7) In Luke 13:15 Christ calls the leader of the synagogue a "hypocrite." In verse 32 He refers to Herod as that "fox." Why are these instances of "name-calling" not sin?

_____

_____

_____

_____

8) Why are Christ's words about money in Luke 12:13–21 so appropriate for our generation today? What does Jesus mean when He says, "For where your treasure is, there your heart will be also" (v. 34 NKJV)?

_____

_____

_____

_____

9) In John 14–17, Jesus prays for unity and harmony. But in Luke 12:49–53, He talked about coming to earth to bring "division" (NKJV). How do we reconcile these passages?

_____

_____

_____

_____

TRUTH FOR TODAY

When speaking of genuine salvation, Jesus made an apt comparison to the characteristics of young children. To be saved, you must come to Christ with the dependent attitude and outlook of a little child: simple, helpless, trusting, unaffected, unpretentious, and unambitious. It's not that children are without sin, but that they are naive and unassuming, dependent on others, and free from selfish claims to grandeur. They submit to the care of their parents and other loved ones, relying on them to meet all their needs. That's the kind of humble and dependent attitude anyone must have who seeks to enter the kingdom of Jesus Christ.

Reflecting on the Text

10) Is your faith like the Pharisees'? Or like a child's? Explain.

_____

_____

_____

11) Do your prayers follow (even loosely) the outline that Christ gave in Luke 11:1–4? What are your biggest obstacles to being more faithful and more effective in the area of prayer?

_____

_____

_____

12) Jesus charged His disciples in Luke 12:31 to "seek the kingdom of God." What does this look like when it is lived out in your life today? Give some specific answers.

_____

_____

_____

Personal Response

Write out additional reflections, questions you may have, or a prayer.

_____

_____

_____

_____

_____

_____

_____

_____

7

CHRIST'S LESSONS AND PARABLES, PART 1

DRAWING NEAR

When was the last time you got excited about someone else coming to faith in Christ? Why did it make you happy?

_____

_____

_____

_____

What does it mean to you that God is your Father?

_____

_____

_____

THE CONTEXT

As Jesus continues His itinerant ministry, He heals a man on the Sabbath, providing Him with another opportunity to challenge the empty religious externalism of Israel's leaders. Knowing that He is headed for a final showdown with these false shepherds, which will end with His own crucifixion, Christ instructs His followers concerning a number of important subjects, including some strong words of discipleship.

Here the master storyteller uses several parables to teach powerful kingdom truths, mainly that our salvation brings great joy to heaven! This section ends with the parable of the unjust steward, directed to Christ's disciples, and the story of the rich man and Lazarus, told for the benefit of the Pharisees. Christ's point in telling this grim account of heaven and hell is to show that unbelief is at heart a moral, not an intellectual, problem.

KEYS TO THE TEXT

Parables: A parable is a long analogy, often cast in the form of a story. These stories were a common form of teaching in Judaism. Before this point in His ministry, Jesus had employed many graphic analogies, but their meaning was fairly clear in the context of His teaching. Parables required more explanation, and Jesus employed them to obscure the truth from unbelievers while making it clearer to His disciples. For the remainder of His Galilean ministry, He did not speak to the multitudes except in parables. Jesus' veiling the truth from unbelievers this way was both an act of judgment and an act of mercy. It was "judgment" because it kept them in the darkness that they loved (see John 3:19), but it was "mercy" because they had already rejected the light, so any exposure to more truth would only increase their condemnation.

The parable of the prodigal son is the most familiar and beloved of all Christ's parables. Unlike most parables, it has more than one lesson. The prodigal is an example of sound repentance. The elder brother illustrates the wickedness of the Pharisees' self-righteousness, prejudice, and indifference toward repenting sinners. And the father pictures God, eager to forgive, and longing for the return of the sinner. The main feature, however, as in the other two parables in this chapter, is the joy of God and the celebrations that fill heaven when a sinner repents.

UNLEASHING THE TEXT

Read 14:1–16:31, noting the key words and definitions next to the passage.

Luke 14:1–16:31 (NKJV)

Sabbath (v. 1)—Christ seems to have favored the Sabbath as a day for doing acts of mercy.

dropsy (v. 1)—a condition in which fluid is retained in the tissues and cavities of the body—often caused by kidney or liver ailments, including cancer

a donkey or an ox (v. 5)—Common humanitarianism (not to mention economic necessity) taught them that it was right to show mercy to animals on the Sabbath; should not the same principles be applied in showing mercy to suffering people?

1 *Now it happened, as He went into the house of one of the rulers of the Pharisees to eat bread on the Sabbath, that they watched Him closely.*

2 *And behold, there was a certain man before Him who had dropsy.*

3 *And Jesus, answering, spoke to the lawyers and Pharisees, saying, "Is it lawful to heal on the Sabbath?"*

4 *But they kept silent. And He took him and healed him, and let him go.*

5 *Then He answered them, saying, "Which of you, having a donkey or an ox that has fallen into a pit, will not immediately pull him out on the Sabbath day?"*

6 *And they could not answer Him regarding these things.*

7 *So He told a parable to those who were invited, when He noted how they chose the best places, saying to them:*

8 *"When you are invited by anyone to a wedding feast, do not sit down in the best place, lest one more honorable than you be invited by him;*

9 *and he who invited you and him come and say to you, 'Give place to this man,' and then you begin with shame to take the lowest place.*

10 *But when you are invited, go and sit down in the lowest place, so that when he who invited you comes he may say to you, 'Friend, go up higher.' Then you will have glory in the presence of those who sit at the table with you.*

11 *For whoever exalts himself will be humbled, and he who humbles himself will be exalted."*

12 *Then He also said to him who invited Him, "When you give a dinner or a supper, do not ask your friends, your brothers, your relatives, nor rich neighbors, lest they also invite you back, and you be repaid.*

13 *But when you give a feast, invite the poor, the maimed, the lame, the blind.*

14 *And you will be blessed, because they cannot repay you; for you shall be repaid at the resurrection of the just."*

15 *Now when one of those who sat at the table with Him heard these things, he said to Him, "Blessed is he who shall eat bread in the kingdom of God!"*

16 *Then He said to him, "A certain man gave a great supper and invited many,*

17 *and sent his servant at supper time to say to those who were invited, 'Come, for all things are now ready.'*

18 *But they all with one accord began to make excuses. The first said to him, 'I have bought a piece of ground, and I must go and see it. I ask you to have me excused.'*

do not ask your friends, your brothers (v. 12)—Such hyperbolic language is common in Semitic discourse and is used for emphasis. The point here is that inviting one's friends and relatives cannot be classified as a spiritual act of true charity.

those who are invited (v. 17)—Guests for a wedding, which could last a full week, were preinvited and given a general idea of the time. When all the many preparations were finally ready, the preinvited guests were notified that the event would commence. Here the preinvited guests refer to the people of Israel, who by the Old Testament had been told to be ready for the arrival of the Messiah.

excuses (v. 18)—All the excuses are insincere. None of these circumstances should have kept the people who were invited from attending the banquet.

the poor and the maimed and the lame and the blind (v. 21)—i.e., people the Pharisees tended to regard as unclean or unworthy

still there is room (v. 22)—God is more willing to save sinners than sinners are to be saved.

great multitudes (v. 25)—Christ's aim was not to gather appreciative crowds, but to make true disciples.

hate (v. 26)—The "hatred" called for here is actually a lesser love. Jesus was calling His disciples to cultivate such a devotion to Him that their attachment to everything else—including their own lives—would seem like hatred by comparison.

forsake all (v. 33)—Only those willing to carefully assess the cost (vv. 28–32) and invest all they had in His kingdom were worthy to enter; it is an absolute, unconditional surrender.

19 *And another said, 'I have bought five yoke of oxen, and I am going to test them. I ask you to have me excused.'*

20 *Still another said, 'I have married a wife, and therefore I cannot come.'*

21 *So that servant came and reported these things to his master. Then the master of the house, being angry, said to his servant, 'Go out quickly into the streets and lanes of the city, and bring in here the poor and the maimed and the lame and the blind.'*

22 *And the servant said, 'Master, it is done as you commanded, and still there is room.'*

23 *Then the master said to the servant, 'Go out into the highways and hedges, and compel them to come in, that my house may be filled.*

24 *For I say to you that none of those men who were invited shall taste my supper.'"*

25 *Now great multitudes went with Him. And He turned and said to them,*

26 *"If anyone comes to Me and does not hate his father and mother, wife and children, brothers and sisters, yes, and his own life also, he cannot be My disciple.*

27 *And whoever does not bear his cross and come after Me cannot be My disciple.*

28 *For which of you, intending to build a tower, does not sit down first and count the cost, whether he has enough to finish it—*

29 *lest, after he has laid the foundation, and is not able to finish, all who see it begin to mock him,*

30 *saying, 'This man began to build and was not able to finish.'*

31 *Or what king, going to make war against another king, does not sit down first and consider whether he is able with ten thousand to meet him who comes against him with twenty thousand?*

32 *Or else, while the other is still a great way off, he sends a delegation and asks conditions of peace.*

33 *So likewise, whoever of you does not forsake all that he has cannot be My disciple.*

34 "Salt is good; but if the salt has lost its flavor, how shall it be seasoned?

35 It is neither fit for the land nor for the dunghill, but men throw it out. He who has ears to hear, let him hear!"

15:1 Then all the tax collectors and the sinners drew near to Him to hear Him.

2 And the Pharisees and scribes complained, saying, "This Man receives sinners and eats with them."

3 So He spoke this parable to them, saying:

4 "What man of you, having a hundred sheep, if he loses one of them, does not leave the ninety-nine in the wilderness, and go after the one which is lost until he finds it?

5 And when he has found it, he lays it on his shoulders, rejoicing.

6 And when he comes home, he calls together his friends and neighbors, saying to them, 'Rejoice with me, for I have found my sheep which was lost!'

7 I say to you that likewise there will be more joy in heaven over one sinner who repents than over ninety-nine just persons who need no repentance.

8 "Or what woman, having ten silver coins, if she loses one coin, does not light a lamp, sweep the house, and search carefully until she finds it?

9 And when she has found it, she calls her friends and neighbors together, saying, 'Rejoice with me, for I have found the piece which I lost!'

10 Likewise, I say to you, there is joy in the presence of the angels of God over one sinner who repents."

11 Then He said: "A certain man had two sons.

12 And the younger of them said to his father, 'Father, give me the portion of goods that falls to me.' So he divided to them his livelihood.

13 And not many days after, the younger son gathered all together, journeyed to a far country, and there wasted his possessions with prodigal living.

14 But when he had spent all, there arose a severe famine in that land, and he began to be in want.

the tax collectors and the sinners (15:1)—The outcasts of society were drawn to Christ, while the religious leaders grew more and more determined to kill Him.

go after the one which is lost (v. 4)—The rabbis taught that God would receive sinners who sought His forgiveness earnestly enough, but here God is the One seeking the sinner.

joy in heaven (v. 7)—This is a reference to the joy of God Himself. There was complaining on earth, among the Pharisees (v. 2), but there was great joy with God and among the angels (v. 10).

give me the portion of goods that falls to me (v. 12)—The son makes a shocking request, tantamount to saying he wished his father were dead. He was not entitled to any inheritance while his father still lived.

prodigal living (v. 13)—He not only exhibited wasteful extravagance, but also wanton immorality (v. 30). The Greek word for *prodigal* means "dissolute" and conveys the idea of an utterly debauched lifestyle.

came to himself (v. 17)—He came to his senses. When his incessant sinning had left him utterly bankrupt and hungry, he was able to think more clearly; in that condition, he was a candidate for salvation.

his father saw him. (v. 20)—Clearly, the father had been waiting and looking for his son's return.

the fatted calf (v. 25)—Reserved only for the most special of occasions, this was a sacrifice or a feast of great celebration, symbolic of the lavishness of salvation's blessings.

older son (v. 25)—He symbolizes the Pharisee, the hypocritical religious person, who stays close to the place of the Father (the temple) but has no sense of sin, no real love for the Father (so as to share in His joy), and no interest in repenting sinners.

15 *Then he went and joined himself to a citizen of that country, and he sent him into his fields to feed swine.*

16 *And he would gladly have filled his stomach with the pods that the swine ate, and no one gave him anything.*

17 *"But when he came to himself, he said, 'How many of my father's hired servants have bread enough and to spare, and I perish with hunger!*

18 *I will arise and go to my father, and will say to him, "Father, I have sinned against heaven and before you,*

19 *and I am no longer worthy to be called your son. Make me like one of your hired servants." '*

20 *"And he arose and came to his father. But when he was still a great way off, his father saw him and had compassion, and ran and fell on his neck and kissed him.*

21 *And the son said to him, 'Father, I have sinned against heaven and in your sight, and am no longer worthy to be called your son.'*

22 *"But the father said to his servants, 'Bring out the best robe and put it on him, and put a ring on his hand and sandals on his feet.*

23 *And bring the fatted calf here and kill it, and let us eat and be merry;*

24 *for this my son was dead and is alive again; he was lost and is found.' And they began to be merry.*

25 *"Now his older son was in the field. And as he came and drew near to the house, he heard music and dancing.*

26 *So he called one of the servants and asked what these things meant.*

27 *And he said to him, 'Your brother has come, and because he has received him safe and sound, your father has killed the fatted calf.'*

28 *"But he was angry and would not go in. Therefore his father came out and pleaded with him.*

29 *So he answered and said to his father, 'Lo, these many years I have been serving you; I never*

transgressed your commandment at any time; and yet you never gave me a young goat, that I might make merry with my friends.

30 *But as soon as this son of yours came, who has devoured your livelihood with harlots, you killed the fatted calf for him.'*

31 *"And he said to him, 'Son, you are always with me, and all that I have is yours.*

32 *It was right that we should make merry and be glad, for your brother was dead and is alive again, and was lost and is found.' "*

16:1 *He also said to His disciples: "There was a certain rich man who had a steward, and an accusation was brought to him that this man was wasting his goods.*

2 *So he called him and said to him, 'What is this I hear about you? Give an account of your stewardship, for you can no longer be steward.'*

3 *"Then the steward said within himself, 'What shall I do? For my master is taking the stewardship away from me. I cannot dig; I am ashamed to beg.*

4 *I have resolved what to do, that when I am put out of the stewardship, they may receive me into their houses.'*

5 *"So he called every one of his master's debtors to him, and said to the first, 'How much do you owe my master?'*

6 *And he said, 'A hundred measures of oil.' So he said to him, 'Take your bill, and sit down quickly and write fifty.'*

7 *Then he said to another, 'And how much do you owe?' So he said, 'A hundred measures of wheat.' And he said to him, 'Take your bill, and write eighty.'*

8 *So the master commended the unjust steward because he had dealt shrewdly. For the sons of this world are more shrewd in their generation than the sons of light.*

9 *"And I say to you, make friends for yourselves by unrighteous mammon, that when you fail, they may receive you into an everlasting home.*

this son of yours (v. 30)—The elder son uses an expression of deep contempt (see "this tax collector" in 18:11). He could not bring himself to refer to him as "my brother."

all that I have is yours (v. 31)—The Pharisees and scribes had easy access to all the riches of God's truth; they spent their lives dealing with Scripture and public worship—but they never really possessed any of the treasures enjoyed by the repentant sinner.

steward (16:1)—A steward was a trusted servant, chief of the management and distribution of household provisions; he acted as an agent for his master, with full authority to transact business in the master's name.

more shrewd (v. 8)—Most unbelievers are wiser in the ways of the world than some believers are toward the things of God.

95

true riches (v. 11)—Faithful use of one's earthly wealth is repeatedly tied to the accumulation of treasure in heaven.

You cannot serve God and mammon (v. 13)—Many of the Pharisees taught that devotion to money and devotion to God were perfectly compatible; while not condemning wealth per se, Christ denounced both love of wealth and devotion to mammon.

everyone is pressing into it (v. 16)—While the Pharisees were busy opposing Christ, sinners were entering His kingdom in droves, with zeal.

than for one tittle of the law to fail (v. 17)—The great moral principles of the Law, the eternal truths contained in the Law's types and symbols, and the promises recorded by the prophets all remain in force and are not abrogated by the kingdom's message.

Abraham's bosom (v. 22)—This same expression (found only here in Scripture) was used in the Talmud as a figure for heaven.

10 *He who is faithful in what is least is faithful also in much; and he who is unjust in what is least is unjust also in much.*

11 *Therefore if you have not been faithful in the unrighteous mammon, who will commit to your trust the true riches?*

12 *And if you have not been faithful in what is another man's, who will give you what is your own?*

13 *"No servant can serve two masters; for either he will hate the one and love the other, or else he will be loyal to the one and despise the other. You cannot serve God and mammon."*

14 *Now the Pharisees, who were lovers of money, also heard all these things, and they derided Him.*

15 *And He said to them, "You are those who justify yourselves before men, but God knows your hearts. For what is highly esteemed among men is an abomination in the sight of God.*

16 *"The law and the prophets were until John. Since that time the kingdom of God has been preached, and everyone is pressing into it.*

17 *And it is easier for heaven and earth to pass away than for one tittle of the law to fail.*

18 *"Whoever divorces his wife and marries another commits adultery; and whoever marries her who is divorced from her husband commits adultery.*

19 *"There was a certain rich man who was clothed in purple and fine linen and fared sumptuously every day.*

20 *But there was a certain beggar named Lazarus, full of sores, who was laid at his gate,*

21 *desiring to be fed with the crumbs which fell from the rich man's table. Moreover the dogs came and licked his sores.*

22 *So it was that the beggar died, and was carried by the angels to Abraham's bosom. The rich man also died and was buried.*

23 *And being in torments in Hades, he lifted up his eyes and saw Abraham afar off, and Lazarus in his bosom.*

24 "Then he cried and said, 'Father Abraham, have mercy on me, and send Lazarus that he may dip the tip of his finger in water and cool my tongue; for I am tormented in this flame.'

25 But Abraham said, 'Son, remember that in your lifetime you received your good things, and likewise Lazarus evil things; but now he is comforted and you are tormented.

26 And besides all this, between us and you there is a great gulf fixed, so that those who want to pass from here to you cannot, nor can those from there pass to us.'

27 "Then he said, 'I beg you therefore, father, that you would send him to my father's house,

28 for I have five brothers, that he may testify to them, lest they also come to this place of torment.'

29 Abraham said to him, 'They have Moses and the prophets; let them hear them.'

30 And he said, 'No, father Abraham; but if one goes to them from the dead, they will repent.'

31 But he said to him, 'If they do not hear Moses and the prophets, neither will they be persuaded though one rise from the dead.' "

I am tormented (v. 24)—Christ pictured Hades as a place where the unspeakable torment of hell had already begun.

neither will they be persuaded (v. 31)—This speaks powerfully of the singular sufficiency of Scripture to overcome unbelief.

1) List the dominant themes found in Luke 14. What ideas or truths does Christ seem to be emphasizing here?

_____

_____

_____

_____

2) Summarize Jesus' teaching on discipleship in Luke 14:25–34.

_____

_____

_____

_____

3) Luke 15 contains one of the most beloved stories Christ ever told—the parable of the prodigal son. Take a few minutes to carefully describe each of the main characters:

⟿ The younger son

___

⟿ The father

___

⟿ The older son

___

4) In Luke 16, we find Jesus' parable of the shrewd manager. What is Jesus' point here?

___

___

___

5) Who is the story of the rich man and Lazarus told for? What is the message?

___

___

___

GOING DEEPER

Jesus had much to say about our attitude toward mammon—wealth. For more insight, read 1 Timothy 6:7–10, 17–19.

7 *For we brought nothing into this world, and it is certain we can carry nothing out.*

8 *And having food and clothing, with these we shall be content.*

9 *But those who desire to be rich fall into temptation and a snare, and into many foolish and harmful lusts which drown men in destruction and perdition.*

10 *For the love of money is a root of all kinds of evil, for which some have strayed from the faith in their greediness, and pierced themselves through with many sorrows . . .*

17 *Command those who are rich in this present age not to be haughty, nor to trust in uncertain riches but in the living God, who gives us richly all things to enjoy.*

18 *Let them do good, that they be rich in good works, ready to give, willing to share,*

19 *storing up for themselves a good foundation for the time to come, that they may lay hold on eternal life.*

EXPLORING THE MEANING

6) Combining Paul's words to Timothy with Jesus' warnings in Luke 16:9–15, what conclusions can you draw about worldly wealth?

_____

_____

_____

7) Many false gods in non-Christian religions are indifferent or even hostile to mankind. Contrast this with the father in the prodigal son (representative of God the Father). What does this story suggest about God's attitude toward repentant sinners?

_____

_____

_____

8) Luke 14:25 speaks of the large crowds that were following Jesus. Why, then, would Christ speak hard words that would very likely turn many away (vv. 26–34)?

_____

_____

_____

9) In what ways were the Pharisees and scribes of Jesus' day like the older brother in the parable of the prodigal son?

_____

_____

_____

TRUTH FOR TODAY

Salvation does not come by confirmation, communion, baptism, church membership, church attendance, trying to keep the Ten Commandments, or living out the

Sermon on the Mount. It does not come by giving to charity or even by believing that there is a God. It does not come by simply being moral and respectable. Salvation does not even come by claiming to be a Christian. Salvation comes only when we receive by faith the gift of God's grace. Hell will be full of people who tried to reach heaven some other way. Dr. Donald Grey Barnhouse said, "Love that goes upward is worship; love that goes outward is affection; love that stoops is grace." God has stooped to give us grace. Will you receive it?

REFLECTING ON THE TEXT

10) What are some ways the "Pharisaical spirit" is still alive today in churches? Why is grace so offensive to so many people?

_____

_____

_____

11) The life that Christ proposed for His followers never involved "convenience" or "comfort." Look again at Luke 14. Put your life up against Christ's un-flinching call. Would you say you are following Jesus with your whole heart?

_____

_____

_____

12) List two things that, with God's help, you will begin to change today.

_____

_____

_____

PERSONAL RESPONSE

Write out additional reflections, questions you may have, or a prayer.

_____

_____

_____

_____

_____

~8~
CHRIST'S LESSONS AND PARABLES, PART 2

Luke 17:1–18:34

DRAWING NEAR

How would you define "faith" to a child?

_____

_____

_____

How would you define "faith" to an adult?

_____

_____

_____

THE CONTEXT

Israel's leaders, threatened by Christ's popularity and authority, were violently opposed to His teaching. Meanwhile, the masses, enamored with the supernatural power of Jesus, were content to enjoy His blessings, without committing to His high standards of discipleship. Still ministering in the region of Perea, Luke 17 and 18 reveal a final series of lessons and parables to all who have ears to hear. Jesus taught about forgiveness, faithfulness, thankfulness, and readiness. Chapter 18 begins with two parables: the parable of the persistent widow and the parable of the Pharisee and the publican. The chapter ends with three rapid-fire lessons about childlikeness, commitment, and the plan of redemption. As you "sit in" on these wonderful lessons, listen with a humble heart.

KEYS TO THE TEXT

Kingdom of God: Jesus made it clear that He was bringing in an altogether different kind of kingdom, which was manifest through the rule of God in men's hearts through faith in the Savior (Luke 17:20–21). This kingdom was neither confined to a particular geographical location nor visible to human eyes. It would come quietly, invisibly, and without the normal pomp and splendor associated with the arrival of a king. This kingdom was about serving, not power. Jesus did not suggest that the Old Testament promises of an earthly kingdom were hereby nullified. Rather, that earthly, visible manifestation of the kingdom is yet to come.

Faith: This term is from the Greek word *pistis,* meaning "trust" or "belief." To have faith is to relinquish trust in oneself and transfer that trust to someone or something else. Within the Epistles, the word *pistis* sometimes refers to the content of one's faith and beliefs—God's revelation in the Scripture. True faith, by Christ's definition, always involves surrender to the will of God. What He was teaching here is nothing like positive-thinking psychology. He was saying that both the source and the object of all genuine faith—even the weak, mustard-seed variety—is God. And "with God nothing will be impossible" (Luke 1:37 NKJV).

UNLEASHING THE TEXT

Read 17:1–18:34, noting the key words and definitions next to the passage.

Luke 17:1–18:34 (NKJV)

1 Then He said to the disciples, "It is impossible that no offenses should come, but woe to him through whom they do come!

little ones (v. 2)—believers; God's children who are under His care

2 It would be better for him if a millstone were hung around his neck, and he were thrown into the sea, than that he should offend one of these little ones.

rebuke him (v. 3)—It is the Christian's duty to deal straightforwardly with a brother or sister in sin.

3 Take heed to yourselves. If your brother sins against you, rebuke him; and if he repents, forgive him.

seven times in a day (v. 4)—i.e., no matter how many times he sins and repents

4 And if he sins against you seven times in a day, and seven times in a day returns to you, saying, 'I repent,' you shall forgive him."

"Increase our faith" (v. 5)—Literally, "Give us more faith." They felt inadequate in the face of the high standard He set for them.

5 And the apostles said to the Lord, "Increase our faith."

6 So the Lord said, "If you have faith as a mustard seed, you can say to this mulberry tree, 'Be pulled up by the roots and be planted in the sea,' and it would obey you.

7 And which of you, having a servant plowing or tending sheep, will say to him when he has come in from the field, 'Come at once and sit down to eat'?

8 But will he not rather say to him, 'Prepare

something for my supper, and gird yourself and serve me till I have eaten and drunk, and afterward you will eat and drink'?

9 Does he thank that servant because he did the things that were commanded him? I think not.

10 So likewise you, when you have done all those things which you are commanded, say, 'We are unprofitable servants. We have done what was our duty to do.' "

unprofitable servants (v. 10)—i.e., not worthy of any special honor

11 Now it happened as He went to Jerusalem that He passed through the midst of Samaria and Galilee.

12 Then as He entered a certain village, there met Him ten men who were lepers, who stood afar off.

13 And they lifted up their voices and said, "Jesus, Master, have mercy on us!"

14 So when He saw them, He said to them, "Go, show yourselves to the priests." And so it was that as they went, they were cleansed.

show yourselves to the priests (v. 14)—i.e., to be declared clean (Lev. 13:2, 3; 14:2–32)

15 And one of them, when he saw that he was healed, returned, and with a loud voice glorified God,

16 and fell down on his face at His feet, giving Him thanks. And he was a Samaritan.

17 So Jesus answered and said, "Were there not ten cleansed? But where are the nine?

18 Were there not any found who returned to give glory to God except this foreigner?"

19 And He said to him, "Arise, go your way. Your faith has made you well."

20 Now when He was asked by the Pharisees when the kingdom of God would come, He answered them and said, "The kingdom of God does not come with observation;

21 nor will they say, 'See here!' or 'See there!' For indeed, the kingdom of God is within you."

within you (v. 21)—i.e., within people's hearts. The pronoun could hardly refer to the Pharisees in general.

22 Then He said to the disciples, "The days will come when you will desire to see one of the days of the Son of Man, and you will not see it.

23 And they will say to you, 'Look here!' or 'Look there!' Do not go after them or follow them.

must suffer (v. 25)—because it was the sovereign plan of God for Him to die as a substitute for sinners (see 9:22; 18:31–33; 24:25, 26; Matt. 16:21; Mark 8:31)

24 *For as the lightning that flashes out of one part under heaven shines to the other part under heaven, so also the Son of Man will be in His day.*

25 *But first He must suffer many things and be rejected by this generation.*

26 *And as it was in the days of Noah, so it will be also in the days of the Son of Man:*

27 *They ate, they drank, they married wives, they were given in marriage, until the day that Noah entered the ark, and the flood came and destroyed them all.*

28 *Likewise as it was also in the days of Lot: They ate, they drank, they bought, they sold, they planted, they built;*

29 *but on the day that Lot went out of Sodom it rained fire and brimstone from heaven and destroyed them all.*

30 *Even so will it be in the day when the Son of Man is revealed.*

housetop (v. 31)—The typical house had a flat roof with an external stairway; the danger would be so great that those on the roofs should flee, without going into the house to retrieve anything.

31 *"In that day, he who is on the housetop, and his goods are in the house, let him not come down to take them away. And likewise the one who is in the field, let him not turn back.*

32 *Remember Lot's wife.*

33 *Whoever seeks to save his life will lose it, and whoever loses his life will preserve it.*

34 *I tell you, in that night there will be two men in one bed: the one will be taken and the other will be left.*

35 *Two women will be grinding together: the one will be taken and the other left.*

36 *Two men will be in the field: the one will be taken and the other left."*

37 *And they answered and said to Him, "Where, Lord?" So He said to them, "Wherever the body is, there the eagles will be gathered together."*

not lose heart (18:1)—in light of the afflictions and hardships of life, and the evidence of approaching judgment

18:1 *Then He spoke a parable to them, that men always ought to pray and not lose heart,*

2 *saying: "There was in a certain city a judge who did not fear God nor regard man.*

3 *Now there was a widow in that city; and she came to him, saying, 'Get justice for me from my adversary.'*

4 *And he would not for a while; but afterward he said within himself, 'Though I do not fear God nor regard man,*

5 *yet because this widow troubles me I will avenge her, lest by her continual coming she weary me.' "*

6 *Then the Lord said, "Hear what the unjust judge said.*

7 *And shall God not avenge His own elect who cry out day and night to Him, though He bears long with them?*

8 *I tell you that He will avenge them speedily. Nevertheless, when the Son of Man comes, will He really find faith on the earth?"*

9 *Also He spoke this parable to some who trusted in themselves that they were righteous, and despised others:*

10 *"Two men went up to the temple to pray, one a Pharisee and the other a tax collector.*

11 *The Pharisee stood and prayed thus with himself, 'God, I thank You that I am not like other men— extortioners, unjust, adulterers, or even as this tax collector.*

12 *I fast twice a week; I give tithes of all that I possess.'*

13 *And the tax collector, standing afar off, would not so much as raise his eyes to heaven, but beat his breast, saying, 'God, be merciful to me a sinner!'*

14 *I tell you, this man went down to his house justified rather than the other; for everyone who exalts himself will be humbled, and he who humbles himself will be exalted."*

15 *Then they also brought infants to Him that He might touch them; but when the disciples saw it, they rebuked them.*

16 *But Jesus called them to Him and said, "Let the little children come to Me, and do not forbid them; for of such is the kingdom of God.*

weary me (v. 5)—Literally, "hit under the eye." What the judge would not do out of compassion for the widow or reverence for God, he would do out of sheer frustration with her incessant pleading.

Will He really find faith? (v. 8)— This suggests that when He returns, the true faith will be comparatively rare—as in the days of Noah (17:26), when only eight souls were saved. The period before His return will be marked by persecution, apostasy, and unbelief (Matt. 24:9–13, 24).

fast twice a week (v. 12)—This is more than is required by any biblical standard. By exalting his own works, the Pharisee revealed that his entire hope lay in his not being as bad as someone else.

justified (v. 14)—i.e., reckoned righteous before God by means of an imputed righteousness

17 *Assuredly, I say to you, whoever does not receive the kingdom of God as a little child will by no means enter it."*

18 *Now a certain ruler asked Him, saying, "Good Teacher, what shall I do to inherit eternal life?"*

19 *So Jesus said to him, "Why do you call Me good? No one is good but One, that is, God.*

20 *You know the commandments: 'Do not commit adultery,' 'Do not murder,' 'Do not steal,' 'Do not bear false witness,' 'Honor your father and your mother.' "*

21 *And he said, "All these things I have kept from my youth."*

22 *So when Jesus heard these things, He said to him, "You still lack one thing. Sell all that you have and distribute to the poor, and you will have treasure in heaven; and come, follow Me."*

23 *But when he heard this, he became very sorrowful, for he was very rich.*

24 *And when Jesus saw that he became very sorrowful, He said, "How hard it is for those who have riches to enter the kingdom of God!*

25 *For it is easier for a camel to go through the eye of a needle than for a rich man to enter the kingdom of God."*

26 *And those who heard it said, "Who then can be saved?"*

27 *But He said, "The things which are impossible with men are possible with God."*

28 *Then Peter said, "See, we have left all and followed You."*

29 *So He said to them, "Assuredly, I say to you, there is no one who has left house or parents or brothers or wife or children, for the sake of the kingdom of God,*

30 *who shall not receive many times more in this present time, and in the age to come eternal life."*

31 *Then He took the twelve aside and said to them, "Behold, we are going up to Jerusalem, and all things that are written by the prophets concerning the Son of Man will be accomplished.*

32 *For He will be delivered to the Gentiles and will be mocked and insulted and spit upon.*

33 *They will scourge Him and kill Him. And the third day He will rise again."*

34 *But they understood none of these things; this saying was hidden from them, and they did not know the things which were spoken.*

they did not know (v. 34)— The whole matter of Christ's death and resurrection was not grasped by the Twelve; they were enamored with other ideas about the Messiah and how His earthly rule would operate.

1) Summarize Jesus' teaching on forgiveness in Luke 17:1–4.

2) How did Jesus respond to the disciples' request to increase their faith (17:5)?

3) Summarize what happens in the parable Jesus told in Luke 17:7–10. What is the point?

4) Describe the characters in the parable of the unjust judge (18:2).

5) To what audience did Jesus direct the parable of the Pharisee and the tax collector? Why?

Going Deeper

Jesus often cited Old Testament allusions in His teaching. For more insight about Lot, read Genesis 19:1–26.

1 *Now the two angels came to Sodom in the evening, and Lot was sitting in the gate of Sodom. When Lot saw them, he rose to meet them, and he bowed himself with his face toward the ground.*

2 *And he said, "Here now, my lords, please turn in to your servant's house and spend the night, and wash your feet; then you may rise early and go on your way." And they said, "No, but we will spend the night in the open square."*

3 *But he insisted strongly; so they turned in to him and entered his house. Then he made them a feast, and baked unleavened bread, and they ate.*

4 *Now before they lay down, the men of the city, the men of Sodom, both old and young, all the people from every quarter, surrounded the house.*

5 *And they called to Lot and said to him, "Where are the men who came to you tonight? Bring them out to us that we may know them carnally."*

6 *So Lot went out to them through the doorway, shut the door behind him,*

7 *and said, "Please, my brethren, do not do so wickedly!*

8 *See now, I have two daughters who have not known a man; please, let me bring them out to you, and you may do to them as you wish; only do nothing to these men, since this is the reason they have come under the shadow of my roof."*

9 *And they said, "Stand back!" Then they said, "This one came in to stay here, and he keeps acting as a judge; now we will deal worse with you than with them." So they pressed hard against the man Lot, and came near to break down the door.*

10 *But the men reached out their hands and pulled Lot into the house with them, and shut the door.*

11 *And they struck the men who were at the doorway of the house with blindness, both small and great, so that they became weary trying to find the door.*

12 *Then the men said to Lot, "Have you anyone else here? Son-in-law, your sons, your daughters, and whomever you have in the city— take them out of this place!*

13 *For we will destroy this place, because the outcry against them has grown great before the face of the LORD, and the LORD has sent us to destroy it."*

14 *So Lot went out and spoke to his sons-in-law, who had married his daughters, and said, "Get up, get out of this place; for the LORD will destroy this city!" But to his sons-in-law he seemed to be joking.*

15 *When the morning dawned, the angels urged Lot to hurry, saying, "Arise, take your wife and your two daughters who are here, lest you be consumed in the punishment of the city."*

16 *And while he lingered, the men took hold of his hand, his wife's hand, and the hands of his two daughters, the LORD being merciful to him, and they brought him out and set him outside the city.*

17 *So it came to pass, when they had brought them outside, that he said, "Escape for your life! Do not look behind you nor stay anywhere in the plain. Escape to the mountains, lest you be destroyed."*

18 *Then Lot said to them, "Please, no, my lords!*

19 *Indeed now, your servant has found favor in your sight, and you have increased your mercy which you have shown me by saving my life; but I cannot escape to the mountains, lest some evil overtake me and I die.*

20 *See now, this city is near enough to flee to, and it is a little one; please let me escape there (is it not a little one?) and my soul shall live."*

21 *And he said to him, "See, I have favored you concerning this thing also, in that I will not overthrow this city for which you have spoken.*

22 *Hurry, escape there. For I cannot do anything until you arrive there." Therefore the name of the city was called Zoar.*

23 *The sun had risen upon the earth when Lot entered Zoar.*

24 *Then the LORD rained brimstone and fire on Sodom and Gomorrah, from the LORD out of the heavens.*

25 *So He overthrew those cities, all the plain, all the inhabitants of the cities, and what grew on the ground.*

26 *But his wife looked back behind him, and she became a pillar of salt.*

EXPLORING THE MEANING

6) Having read the Old Testament account of Lot, how do you now interpret Christ's terse warning, "Remember Lot's wife" (Luke 17:32)? What is the significance of this exhortation in light of Christ's second coming?

_____

_____

_____

_____

_____

_____

7) What does it mean when Jesus says that the kingdom of God is "within" His followers (17:21)?

_____

_____

_____

8) What is the meaning of the parable of the unjust judge? What would you say to a person who argued that the judge in the story is supposed to represent God?

_____

_____

_____

9) What does Christ's parable of the Pharisee and the tax collector (18:9–14) teach us about:

⟶ Pride/humility?

_____

_____

_____

⟶ Being righteous in God's sight?

_____

_____

_____

⟶ Grace?

_____

_____

_____

TRUTH FOR TODAY

When the rich young ruler approached Jesus concerning salvation, our Lord immediately tested his willingness to deny all and follow Him: "Sell all that you have and distribute to the poor, and you will have treasure in heaven; and come, follow Me" (Luke 18:22 NKJV). When the young ruler did not heed Jesus' words, he revealed an unwillingness to submit to the lordship of Christ.

Anyone who would come to salvation must yield control of his life to the Savior. That means being willing either to give up everything to follow Him, or to be content with all He has given you, with the realization that He may sovereignly give you more as you serve Him. Salvation is the exchange of all that you are for all that Christ is. Saving faith, therefore, is not merely an act of the mind; it counts the cost and humbly cries out to God as did the tax collector in Luke 18:13, "God, be merciful to me a sinner!" (NKJV).

REFLECTING ON THE TEXT

10) In the spirit of the story of the rich young ruler, are you counting the cost today and every day? Is your life yielded fully to Christ? How do you know?

_____

_____

_____

_____

11) Let this passage serve as a kind of "spiritual report card." What kind of marks would you give yourself in the following areas:

⌐ Demonstrating faith

⌐ Thankfulness

⌐ Watchfulness (living in light of the Lord's imminent return)

⌐ Persistence in prayer

⌐ Humility

⌐ The willingness to put Christ above all else

_____

_____

_____

_____

12) Jesus stated this truth, "The things which are impossible with men are possible with God" (18:27 NKJV). What "impossible" situation or relationship or obstacle will you entrust to God today? Ask the Lord to increase your faith.

_____

_____

_____

Personal Response

Write out additional reflections, questions you may have, or a prayer.

_____

_____

_____

_____

_____

_____

_____

_____

_____

_____

_____

_____

_____

_____

_____

_____

_____

_____

_____

～9～
CHRIST UP CLOSE

DRAWING NEAR

Write a sentence expressing your response to each of these names of Christ. Which one means the most to you right now?

⌐ The Great Physician

_____

_____

_____

⌐ The Good Shepherd

_____

_____

_____

⌐ The Savior of the World

_____

_____

_____

⌐ The Friend of Sinners

_____

_____

_____

_____

THE CONTEXT

In this passage we meet Jesus, the Friend of sinners! After he heals blind Bartimaeus, we read the beloved story of Christ showing kindness and mercy to Zacchaeus. This underscores the theme of Luke's gospel: "The Son of Man has come to seek and to save that which was lost" (19:10 NKJV). Next we meet Christ, the Judge of all the earth, through the parable of the ten minas. Then, we meet Christ, the King of kings. He enters Jerusalem on a donkey colt, to the wild

113

cheers of the masses. From there He takes His ministry to the temple, cleansing it of the merchants and moneychangers. He then walks into the very heart of enemy territory, and the opposition leaders are intent on destroying Him.

KEYS TO THE TEXT

Scribes and Chief Priests: The Greek word for *scribe* is *grammateus*, literally, "writer." Originally, scribes functioned as transcribers of the Law and readers of the Scripture. Later they acted as lawyers and religious scholars by interpreting both civil and religious law. The Greek word for *chief priests* translates as "the leading priests." This group included the high priest and other priests who were experts in the Scriptures. Ironically, these priests did not realize that by mocking Jesus they were fulfilling Isaiah's prophecy regarding the Messiah: "He is despised and rejected by men, a Man of sorrows and acquainted with grief" (Isa. 53:3 NKJV).

UNLEASHING THE TEXT

Read 18:35–19:48, noting the key words and definitions next to the passage.

Luke 18:35–19:48 (NKJV)

35 Then it happened, as He was coming near Jericho, that a certain blind man sat by the road begging.

36 And hearing a multitude passing by, he asked what it meant.

37 So they told him that Jesus of Nazareth was passing by.

Son of David (v. 38)—an affirmation that he recognized Jesus as Messiah and King

38 And he cried out, saying, "Jesus, Son of David, have mercy on me!"

39 Then those who went before warned him that he should be quiet; but he cried out all the more, "Son of David, have mercy on me!"

40 So Jesus stood still and commanded him to be brought to Him. And when he had come near, He asked him,

41 saying, "What do you want Me to do for you?" He said, "Lord, that I may receive my sight."

42 Then Jesus said to him, "Receive your sight; your faith has made you well."

43 And immediately he received his sight, and followed Him, glorifying God. And all the people, when they saw it, gave praise to God.

19:1 *Then Jesus entered and passed through Jericho.*

2 *Now behold, there was a man named Zacchaeus who was a chief tax collector, and he was rich.*

3 *And he sought to see who Jesus was, but could not because of the crowd, for he was of short stature.*

4 *So he ran ahead and climbed up into a sycamore tree to see Him, for He was going to pass that way.*

5 *And when Jesus came to the place, He looked up and saw him, and said to him, "Zacchaeus, make haste and come down, for today I must stay at your house."*

6 *So he made haste and came down, and received Him joyfully.*

7 *But when they saw it, they all complained, saying, "He has gone to be a guest with a man who is a sinner."*

8 *Then Zacchaeus stood and said to the Lord, "Look, Lord, I give half of my goods to the poor; and if I have taken anything from anyone by false accusation, I restore fourfold."*

9 *And Jesus said to him, "Today salvation has come to this house, because he also is a son of Abraham;*

10 *for the Son of Man has come to seek and to save that which was lost."*

11 *Now as they heard these things, He spoke another parable, because He was near Jerusalem and because they thought the kingdom of God would appear immediately.*

12 *Therefore He said: "A certain nobleman went into a far country to receive for himself a kingdom and to return.*

13 *So he called ten of his servants, delivered to them ten minas, and said to them, 'Do business till I come.'*

14 *But his citizens hated him, and sent a delegation after him, saying, 'We will not have this man to reign over us.'*

15 *"And so it was that when he returned, having received the kingdom, he then commanded these*

chief tax collector (19:2)—Zacchaeus probably oversaw a large tax district and had other tax collectors working for him.

sycamore tree (v. 4)—This would have been a sturdy tree with low, spreading branches. A small person could get out on a limb and hang over the road; this was an undignified position for someone of Zacchaeus's rank, but he was desperate to see Christ.

joyfully (v. 6)—Such a despicable sinner as a typical tax collector might have been distressed at the prospect of a visit from the perfect, sinless Son of God, but Zacchaeus's heart was prepared.

I restore fourfold (v. 8)—Zacchaeus's willingness to make restitution was proof that his conversion was genuine. It was the fruit, not the condition, of his salvation.

to seek and to save that which was lost (v. 10)—the main theme of Luke's gospel (see 5:31, 32; 15:4–7, 32)

minas (v. 13)—a Greek measure of money, equal to slightly more than three month's salary

when he returned (v. 15)—This pictured Christ's return to earth. The full manifestation of His kingdom on earth awaits that time.

servants, to whom he had given the money, to be called to him, that he might know how much every man had gained by trading.

16 Then came the first, saying, 'Master, your mina has earned ten minas.'

17 And he said to him, 'Well done, good servant; because you were faithful in a very little, have authority over ten cities.'

18 And the second came, saying, 'Master, your mina has earned five minas.'

19 Likewise he said to him, 'You also be over five cities.'

20 "Then another came, saying, 'Master, here is your mina, which I have kept put away in a handkerchief.

I feared you (v. 21)—The servant displays a craven fear, not borne out of love or reverence, but tainted with contempt for the master. Had he had any true regard for the master, a righteous "fear" would have provoked diligence rather than sloth.

21 For I feared you, because you are an austere man. You collect what you did not deposit, and reap what you did not sow.'

22 And he said to him, 'Out of your own mouth I will judge you, you wicked servant. You knew that I was an austere man, collecting what I did not deposit and reaping what I did not sow.

23 Why then did you not put my money in the bank, that at my coming I might have collected it with interest?'

24 "And he said to those who stood by, 'Take the mina from him, and give it to him who has ten minas.'

25 (But they said to him, 'Master, he has ten minas.')

26 'For I say to you, that to everyone who has will be given; and from him who does not have, even what he has will be taken away from him.

27 But bring here those enemies of mine, who did not want me to reign over them, and slay them before me.' "

up to Jerusalem (v. 28)—The road from Jericho to Jerusalem was a steep ascent, rising some 4,000 feet in about 20 miles.

28 When He had said this, He went on ahead, going up to Jerusalem.

29 And it came to pass, when He drew near to Bethphage and Bethany, at the mountain called Olivet, that He sent two of His disciples,

colt (v. 30)—The other Gospels say this was a donkey colt (see Zech. 9:9), and Matthew reveals that the mare was brought along as well.

30 saying, "Go into the village opposite you, where as you enter you will find a colt tied, on which no one has ever sat. Loose it and bring it here.

31 *And if anyone asks you, 'Why are you loosing it?' thus you shall say to him, 'Because the Lord has need of it.' "*

32 *So those who were sent went their way and found it just as He had said to them.*

33 *But as they were loosing the colt, the owners of it said to them, "Why are you loosing the colt?"*

34 *And they said, "The Lord has need of him."*

35 *Then they brought him to Jesus. And they threw their own clothes on the colt, and they set Jesus on him.*

36 *And as He went, many spread their clothes on the road.*

37 *Then, as He was now drawing near the descent of the Mount of Olives, the whole multitude of the disciples began to rejoice and praise God with a loud voice for all the mighty works they had seen,*

38 *saying: " 'Blessed is the King who comes in the name of the LORD!' Peace in heaven and glory in the highest!"*

39 *And some of the Pharisees called to Him from the crowd, "Teacher, rebuke Your disciples."*

40 *But He answered and said to them, "I tell you that if these should keep silent, the stones would immediately cry out."*

41 *Now as He drew near, He saw the city and wept over it,*

42 *saying, "If you had known, even you, especially in this your day, the things that make for your peace! But now they are hidden from your eyes.*

43 *For days will come upon you when your enemies will build an embankment around you, surround you and close you in on every side,*

44 *and level you, and your children within you, to the ground; and they will not leave in you one stone upon another, because you did not know the time of your visitation."*

45 *Then He went into the temple and began to drive out those who bought and sold in it,*

Blessed is the King (v. 38)—Quoting Psalm 118:26, they hailed Jesus as Messiah.

the stones would immediately cry out (v. 44)—This was a strong claim of deity, and perhaps a reference to the words of Habakkuk 2:11. Scripture often speaks of inanimate nature praising God.

and level you (v. 44)—This was literally fulfilled; the Romans utterly demolished the city, temple, residences, and people; men, women, and children were brutally slaughtered by the tens of thousands.

46 *saying to them, "It is written, 'My house is a house*
   of prayer,' but you have made it a 'den of thieves.'"
47 *And He was teaching daily in the temple. But the*
   chief priests, the scribes, and the leaders of the
   people sought to destroy Him,
48 *and were unable to do anything; for all the people*
   were very attentive to hear Him.

1) What happened as Jesus approached Jericho?

_____

_____

2) Who was Zacchaeus? What was his story?

_____

_____

3) How did Zacchaeus respond to his encounter with Jesus?

_____

_____

4) Summarize Jesus' parable of the minas (19:11–27).

‿ Setting:

_____

_____

‿ Characters:

_____

_____

‿ Plot/story:

_____

_____

⁓ Theme:

_____

_____

5) Describe Jesus' actions as He entered Jerusalem.

_____

_____

_____

_____

GOING DEEPER

For another similar parable about stewardship, read Matthew 25:14–30.

14 *"For the kingdom of heaven is like a man traveling to a far country, who called his own servants and delivered his goods to them.*

15 *And to one he gave five talents, to another two, and to another one, to each according to his own ability; and immediately he went on a journey.*

16 *Then he who had received the five talents went and traded with them, and made another five talents.*

17 *And likewise he who had received two gained two more also.*

18 *But he who had received one went and dug in the ground, and hid his lord's money.*

19 *After a long time the lord of those servants came and settled accounts with them.*

20 *"So he who had received five talents came and brought five other talents, saying, 'Lord, you delivered to me five talents; look, I have gained five more talents besides them.'*

21 *His lord said to him, 'Well done, good and faithful servant; you were faithful over a few things, I will make you ruler over many things. Enter into the joy of your lord.'*

22 *He also who had received two talents came and said, 'Lord, you delivered to me two talents; look, I have gained two more talents besides them.'*

23 *His lord said to him, 'Well done, good and faithful servant; you have been faithful over a few things, I will make you ruler over many things. Enter into the joy of your lord.'*

24 *"Then he who had received the one talent came and said, 'Lord, I knew you to be a hard man, reaping where you have not sown, and gathering where you have not scattered seed.*

25 *And I was afraid, and went and hid your talent in the ground. Look, there you have what is yours.'*

26 *"But his lord answered and said to him, 'You wicked and lazy servant, you knew that I reap where I have not sown, and gather where I have not scattered seed.*

27 *So you ought to have deposited my money with the bankers, and at my coming I would have received back my own with interest.*

28 *So take the talent from him, and give it to him who has ten talents.*

29 *'For to everyone who has, more will be given, and he will have abundance; but from him who does not have, even what he has will be taken away.*

30 *And cast the unprofitable servant into the outer darkness. There will be weeping and gnashing of teeth.'"*

Exploring the Meaning

6) What are the similarities between Matthew's parable of the talents (Matt. 25:14–30) and Luke's parable of the minas (Luke 19:11–27)? What are the differences?

_____

_____

_____

_____

7) What are the lessons of the parable of the minas? What does this teaching tell us about working for Christ and His kingdom?

_____

_____

_____

_____

8) In what ways is Luke's story of Zacchaeus a perfect microcosm of Luke's entire gospel, indeed of Christ's entire ministry on earth?

_____

_____

_____

_____

9) Christ entered Jerusalem to great fanfare and hoopla, and Luke records that He then began to weep (19:41). Why?

_____

_____

_____

_____

Truth for Today

Your essential character—your inner motives, convictions, loyalties, and ambitions—will eventually show through in what you say and do. Good works do not save you, but every believer is saved *for* good works. "For we are His workmanship, created in Christ Jesus for good works, which God prepared beforehand that we should walk in them" (Eph. 2:10 NKJV). For the believer, true fruit-bearing occurs with the help of Christ. On the other hand, unbelievers (including those who falsely profess Christ) will eventually demonstrate the bad fruit that their unregenerate lives inevitably produce. If you are bearing fruit, you will be growing in faith, virtue, knowledge, self-control, perseverance, godliness, brotherly kindness, and love (see 2 Pet. 1:5–9).

Reflecting on the Text

10) Zacchaeus demonstrated some radical changes after his encounter with Christ. What fruit do you see in your life? How has Christ changed you?

_____

_____

_____

_____

11) Think of all that God has given you—abilities, strengths, spiritual gifts, life experiences, education/knowledge, relationships, opportunities, material possessions/assets, etc. What are some specific ways you can be a better steward of these resources and blessings?

_____

_____

_____

12) Luke 19:48 says that the people "were very attentive to hear Him." How will you seek to listen more closely to Christ and obey His leading today?

_____

_____

_____

PERSONAL RESPONSE

Write out additional reflections, questions you may have, or a prayer.

_____

_____

_____

_____

_____

_____

_____

_____

_____

_____

_____

_____

_____

_____

_____

_____

_____

_____

_____

CHRIST'S ENEMIES

~ 10 ~

Luke 20:1–22:6

DRAWING NEAR

Some Christians seem to think that believing in Jesus should shield them from harm and trouble. They act surprised when trials or hard times come. Where do you think this notion comes from?

_____

_____

_____

Have you ever been persecuted because of your faith? If so, what happened?

_____

_____

_____

THE CONTEXT

Christ encountered growing opposition from Israel's leaders. In the final week of his earthly life, the Son of Man faced their all-out hostility. Luke 20 and 21 record the events that happened on Tuesday of Christ's "Passion Week." Jesus clashed with the hate-filled religious leaders who questioned His authority. Then He taught the large crowds who made the holy pilgrimage to Jerusalem (and the temple) to celebrate the Passover Feast. Christ's teaching included a stinging parable about wicked vinedressers, an obvious indictment of the Jewish rulers. His teaching also included a brilliant dialogue with various religious leaders who were trying to trap Him with various theological and political questions. While in the temple, Christ noticed a poor woman making a sacrificial gift. He next prophesied the destruction of Jerusalem and taught about the end times. As this passage ends, we see Judas, one of Christ's twelve apostles, joining the Jewish leaders' wicked conspiracy.

KEYS TO THE TEXT

Christ: Many speak of Jesus Christ without realizing that the title *Christ* is actually a confession of faith. From the Greek term *Christos*, it literally means "the Anointed One." The term *Messiah*, the Hebrew equivalent for *Christ*, was used in the Old Testament to refer to prophets, priests, and kings, in the sense that all of them were anointed with oil. This anointing symbolized a consecration for ministry by God. Jesus Christ, as the Anointed One, would be the ultimate Prophet, Priest, and King (Isa. 61:1; John 3:34). With his dramatic confession, "You are the Christ, the Son of the living God" (Matt. 16:16 NKJV), Peter declared his faith in Jesus as the promised Messiah.

UNLEASHING THE TEXT

Read 20:1–22:6, noting the key words and definitions next to the passage.

Luke 20:1–22:6 (NKJV)

chief priests . . . scribes . . . elders (v. 1)—Each of these groups played a unique role in the various attacks that follow; each was also represented in the Sanhedrin, the Jewish council suggesting that the council had met to orchestrate the attack against Him.

1 Now it happened on one of those days, as He taught the people in the temple and preached the gospel, that the chief priests and the scribes, together with the elders, confronted Him

2 and spoke to Him, saying, "Tell us, by what authority are You doing these things? Or who is he who gave You this authority?"

3 But He answered and said to them, "I also will ask you one thing, and answer Me:

4 The baptism of John—was it from heaven or from men?"

'Why then did you not believe him?' (v. 5)—If John was a prophet whose words were true, they ought to believe His testimony about Christ; on the other hand, it would have been political folly for the Pharisees to attack the legitimacy of John the Baptist or deny his authority as a prophet of God. John was enormously popular with the people and a martyr at the hands of the despised Herod.

5 And they reasoned among themselves, saying, "If we say, 'From heaven,' He will say, 'Why then did you not believe him?'

6 But if we say, 'From men,' all the people will stone us, for they are persuaded that John was a prophet."

7 So they answered that they did not know where it was from.

8 And Jesus said to them, "Neither will I tell you by what authority I do these things."

9 Then He began to tell the people this parable: "A certain man planted a vineyard, leased it to vinedressers, and went into a far country for a long time.

10 Now at vintage-time he sent a servant to the vinedressers, that they might give him some of the fruit of the vineyard. But the vinedressers beat him and sent him away empty-handed.

11 *Again he sent another servant; and they beat him also, treated him shamefully, and sent him away empty-handed.*

12 *And again he sent a third; and they wounded him also and cast him out.*

13 *"Then the owner of the vineyard said, 'What shall I do? I will send my beloved son. Probably they will respect him when they see him.'*

14 *But when the vinedressers saw him, they reasoned among themselves, saying, 'This is the heir. Come, let us kill him, that the inheritance may be ours.'*

15 *So they cast him out of the vineyard and killed him. Therefore what will the owner of the vineyard do to them?*

16 *He will come and destroy those vinedressers and give the vineyard to others." And when they heard it they said, "Certainly not!"*

17 *Then He looked at them and said, "What then is this that is written: 'The stone which the builders rejected Has become the chief cornerstone'?*

18 *Whoever falls on that stone will be broken; but on whomever it falls, it will grind him to powder."*

19 *And the chief priests and the scribes that very hour sought to lay hands on Him, but they feared the people—for they knew He had spoken this parable against them.*

20 *So they watched Him, and sent spies who pretended to be righteous, that they might seize on His words, in order to deliver Him to the power and the authority of the governor.*

21 *Then they asked Him, saying, "Teacher, we know that You say and teach rightly, and You do not show personal favoritism, but teach the way of God in truth:*

22 *Is it lawful for us to pay taxes to Caesar or not?"*

23 *But He perceived their craftiness, and said to them, "Why do you test Me?*

24 *Show Me a denarius. Whose image and inscription does it have?" They answered and said, "Caesar's."*

beloved son (v. 13)—The son in the parable is an illustration of Christ.

Whoever falls . . . on whomever it falls (v. 18)—a quotation from Isaiah 8:13–15, which speaks of Jehovah; applied here to Christ

Whose image (v. 24)—Caesar's image on the denarius was one of the main reasons the Jews chafed at the poll tax; since he pretended to be in a position tantamount to deity, the paying of the tax was unlawful worship—and in the minds of many, tantamount to gross idolatry.

25 And He said to them, "Render therefore to Caesar the things that are Caesar's, and to God the things that are God's."

26 But they could not catch Him in His words in the presence of the people. And they marveled at His answer and kept silent.

27 Then some of the Sadducees, who deny that there is a resurrection, came to Him and asked Him,

28 saying: "Teacher, Moses wrote to us that if a man's brother dies, having a wife, and he dies without children, his brother should take his wife and raise up offspring for his brother.

29 Now there were seven brothers. And the first took a wife, and died without children.

30 And the second took her as wife, and he died childless.

31 Then the third took her, and in like manner the seven also; and they left no children, and died.

32 Last of all the woman died also.

33 Therefore, in the resurrection, whose wife does she become? For all seven had her as wife."

34 Jesus answered and said to them, "The sons of this age marry and are given in marriage.

35 But those who are counted worthy to attain that age, and the resurrection from the dead, neither marry nor are given in marriage;

36 nor can they die anymore, for they are equal to the angels and are sons of God, being sons of the resurrection.

37 But even Moses showed in the burning bush passage that the dead are raised, when he called the Lord 'the God of Abraham, the God of Isaac, and the God of Jacob.'

38 For He is not the God of the dead but of the living, for all live to Him."

39 Then some of the scribes answered and said, "Teacher, You have spoken well."

40 But after that they dared not question Him anymore.

41 *And He said to them, "How can they say that the Christ is the Son of David?*

42 *Now David himself said in the Book of Psalms: 'The LORD said to my Lord, "Sit at My right hand,*

43 *Till I make Your enemies Your footstool." '*

44 *Therefore David calls Him 'Lord'; how is He then his Son?"*

45 *Then, in the hearing of all the people, He said to His disciples,*

46 *"Beware of the scribes, who desire to go around in long robes, love greetings in the marketplaces, the best seats in the synagogues, and the best places at feasts,*

47 *who devour widows' houses, and for a pretense make long prayers. These will receive greater condemnation."*

21:1 *And He looked up and saw the rich putting their gifts into the treasury,*

2 *and He saw also a certain poor widow putting in two mites.*

3 *So He said, "Truly I say to you that this poor widow has put in more than all;*

4 *for all these out of their abundance have put in offerings for God, but she out of her poverty put in all the livelihood that she had."*

5 *Then, as some spoke of the temple, how it was adorned with beautiful stones and donations, He said,*

6 *"These things which you see—the days will come in which not one stone shall be left upon another that shall not be thrown down."*

7 *So they asked Him, saying, "Teacher, but when will these things be? And what sign will there be when these things are about to take place?"*

8 *And He said: "Take heed that you not be deceived. For many will come in My name, saying, 'I am He,' and, 'The time has drawn near.' Therefore do not go after them.*

9 *But when you hear of wars and commotions, do not be terrified; for these things must come to pass first, but the end will not come immediately."*

the treasury (21:1)—Thirteen chests with funnel-shaped openings stood in the court of the women; each was labeled for a specific use, and donations were given accordingly.

poor widow (v. 2)—The Greek expression signifies extreme poverty. This woman was desperately poor, and more fit to be a recipient of charity than a donor.

mites (v. 2)—the smallest copper coins in use in Palestine, worth about one-eighth of a cent, but representing all this woman had to live on

out of their abundance (v. 4)—There was nothing sacrificial about their giving.

not a hair (v. 18)—This was not a promise for the preservation of their physical lives, but a guarantee that they would suffer no eternal loss.

the times of the Gentiles (v. 24)—The era from Israel's Babylonians captivity (ca. 586 BC; see 2 Kings 25) to her restoration in the kingdom (Rev. 20:1–6) has been a time during which, in accord with God's purpose, Gentiles have dominated or threatened Jerusalem. The era has also been marked by vast spiritual privileges for the Gentile nations.

there will be signs (v. 25)—The celestial signs and wonders described here immediately precede the return of Christ.

10 Then He said to them, "Nation will rise against nation, and kingdom against kingdom.

11 And there will be great earthquakes in various places, and famines and pestilences; and there will be fearful sights and great signs from heaven.

12 But before all these things, they will lay their hands on you and persecute you, delivering you up to the synagogues and prisons. You will be brought before kings and rulers for My name's sake.

13 But it will turn out for you as an occasion for testimony.

14 Therefore settle it in your hearts not to meditate beforehand on what you will answer;

15 for I will give you a mouth and wisdom which all your adversaries will not be able to contradict or resist.

16 You will be betrayed even by parents and brothers, relatives and friends; and they will put some of you to death.

17 And you will be hated by all for My name's sake.

18 But not a hair of your head shall be lost.

19 By your patience possess your souls.

20 "But when you see Jerusalem surrounded by armies, then know that its desolation is near.

21 Then let those who are in Judea flee to the mountains, let those who are in the midst of her depart, and let not those who are in the country enter her.

22 For these are the days of vengeance, that all things which are written may be fulfilled.

23 But woe to those who are pregnant and to those who are nursing babies in those days! For there will be great distress in the land and wrath upon this people.

24 And they will fall by the edge of the sword, and be led away captive into all nations. And Jerusalem will be trampled by Gentiles until the times of the Gentiles are fulfilled.

25 "And there will be signs in the sun, in the moon, and in the stars; and on the earth distress of nations, with perplexity, the sea and the waves roaring;

26 *men's hearts failing them from fear and the*
expectation of those things which are coming on
the earth, for the powers of the heavens will be
shaken.

27 *Then they will see the Son of Man coming in a cloud*
with power and great glory.

28 *Now when these things begin to happen, look up*
and lift up your heads, because your redemption
draws near."

29 *Then He spoke to them a parable: "Look at the fig*
tree, and all the trees.

30 *When they are already budding, you see and know*
for yourselves that summer is now near.

31 *So you also, when you see these things happening,*
know that the kingdom of God is near.

32 *Assuredly, I say to you, this generation will by no*
means pass away till all things take place.

33 *Heaven and earth will pass away, but My words will*
by no means pass away.

34 *"But take heed to yourselves, lest your hearts be*
weighed down with carousing, drunkenness,
and cares of this life, and that Day come on you
unexpectedly.

that Day (v. 34)—i.e., the day of
His return

35 *For it will come as a snare on all those who dwell on*
the face of the whole earth.

36 *Watch therefore, and pray always that you may be*
counted worthy to escape all these things that will
come to pass, and to stand before the Son of Man."

37 *And in the daytime He was teaching in the temple,*
but at night He went out and stayed on the
mountain called Olivet.

38 *Then early in the morning all the people came to*
Him in the temple to hear Him.

22:1 *Now the Feast of Unleavened Bread drew near,*
which is called Passover.

2 *And the chief priests and the scribes sought how*
they might kill Him, for they feared the people.

for they feared the people
(22:2)—They were therefore
plotting secretly, hoping to
eliminate Him after the Passover season, when Jerusalem
would not be filled with so many
people; but these events occurred according to God's time-
table, not theirs.

3 *Then Satan entered Judas, surnamed Iscariot, who*
was numbered among the twelve.

agreed to give him money (v. 5)—Matthew 26:15 says thirty pieces of silver, the price of a slave (Ex. 21:32).

4 *So he went his way and conferred with the chief priests and captains, how he might betray Him to them.*

5 *And they were glad, and agreed to give him money.*

6 *So he promised and sought opportunity to betray Him to them in the absence of the multitude.*

1) How are the Jewish religious leaders described in Luke 20? What adjectives and phrases do you see?

_____

_____

_____

_____

2) How would you describe Jesus' tone and manner in this chapter? What is the overall atmosphere here?

_____

_____

_____

_____

3) Skim over the parable of the vineyard owner (20:9–16). What is Jesus' point?

_____

_____

_____

4) Summarize Jesus' teaching in these chapters about the following subjects:

⟿ Paying taxes

⟿ Giving

⟿ Living in the end times

_____

_____

_____

5) Do any of Christ's actions or statements in Luke 20:1–22:6 seem especially provocative or surprising to you? Which ones? Why?

GOING DEEPER

Jesus was not afraid to speak against the scribes and Pharisees. For more of Jesus' warnings to them, read Matthew 23:1–28.

1 *Then Jesus spoke to the multitudes and to His disciples,*
2 *saying: "The scribes and the Pharisees sit in Moses' seat.*
3 *Therefore whatever they tell you to observe, that observe and do, but do not do according to their works; for they say, and do not do.*
4 *For they bind heavy burdens, hard to bear, and lay them on men's shoulders; but they themselves will not move them with one of their fingers.*
5 *But all their works they do to be seen by men. They make their phylacteries broad and enlarge the borders of their garments.*
6 *They love the best places at feasts, the best seats in the synagogues,*
7 *greetings in the marketplaces, and to be called by men, 'Rabbi, Rabbi.'*
8 *But you, do not be called 'Rabbi'; for One is your Teacher, the Christ, and you are all brethren.*
9 *Do not call anyone on earth your father; for One is your Father, He who is in heaven.*
10 *And do not be called teachers; for One is your Teacher, the Christ.*
11 *But he who is greatest among you shall be your servant.*
12 *And whoever exalts himself will be humbled, and he who humbles himself will be exalted.*
13 *"But woe to you, scribes and Pharisees, hypocrites! For you shut up the kingdom of heaven against men; for you neither go in yourselves, nor do you allow those who are entering to go in.*
14 *Woe to you, scribes and Pharisees, hypocrites! For you devour widows' houses, and for a pretense make long prayers. Therefore you will receive greater condemnation.*
15 *"Woe to you, scribes and Pharisees, hypocrites! For you travel land and sea to win one proselyte, and when he is won, you make him twice as much a son of hell as yourselves.*

16 *"Woe to you, blind guides, who say, 'Whoever swears by the temple, it is nothing; but whoever swears by the gold of the temple, he is obliged to perform it.'*

17 *Fools and blind! For which is greater, the gold or the temple that sanctifies the gold?*

18 *And, 'Whoever swears by the altar, it is nothing; but whoever swears by the gift that is on it, he is obliged to perform it.'*

19 *Fools and blind! For which is greater, the gift or the altar that sanctifies the gift?*

20 *Therefore he who swears by the altar, swears by it and by all things on it.*

21 *He who swears by the temple, swears by it and by Him who dwells in it.*

22 *And he who swears by heaven, swears by the throne of God and by Him who sits on it.*

23 *"Woe to you, scribes and Pharisees, hypocrites! For you pay tithe of mint and anise and cummin, and have neglected the weightier matters of the law: justice and mercy and faith. These you ought to have done, without leaving the others undone.*

24 *Blind guides, who strain out a gnat and swallow a camel!*

25 *"Woe to you, scribes and Pharisees, hypocrites! For you cleanse the outside of the cup and dish, but inside they are full of extortion and self-indulgence.*

26 *Blind Pharisee, first cleanse the inside of the cup and dish, that the outside of them may be clean also.*

27 *"Woe to you, scribes and Pharisees, hypocrites! For you are like whitewashed tombs which indeed appear beautiful outwardly, but inside are full of dead men's bones and all uncleanness.*

28 *Even so you also outwardly appear righteous to men, but inside you are full of hypocrisy and lawlessness."*

EXPLORING THE MEANING

6) Why was Christ so stern, so angry with the Jewish religious leaders?

_____

_____

_____

_____

_____

7) What were the Jewish leaders' "issues" with Jesus? Why were they infuriated and so committed to destroy Him?

_____

_____

_____

8) Why was the poor widow's offering pleasing to God?

_____

_____

_____

9) How do you know that Jesus' statement in Luke 21:32 could not have been referring to the disciples' generation?

_____

_____

_____

TRUTH FOR TODAY

No one can live for God's glory and be entirely comfortable in this world. You shouldn't be obnoxious or try to be a misfit, but if your life is Christlike, then you will bear some of the reproach He bore. We live in a day when many want to make Christianity easy, but the Bible says it is hard. Many want to make Christians lovable, but God says they'll be persecuted. Christianity must confront the system by being distinct from it. It must expose sin before it can disclose the remedy. Be sure your life reflects your commitment to Christ. That's what will make you distinct from the world.

REFLECTING ON THE TEXT

10) Those who live for Christ will face the same kind of opposition that He faced. "No servant is above his master." How can you prepare for the reproach that is sure to come your way at some point?

_____

_____

_____

11) Christ might have avoided a "show-down" with the Jewish leaders in any number of ways: by staying away from Jerusalem, by "being a nice guy," by looking "for common ground." Instead, He boldly confronted them with God's truth. What is the lesson for you today from Christ's example?

_____

_____

12) What can you take away from the story of the poor widow and her sacrificial giving?

_____

_____

PERSONAL RESPONSE

Write out additional reflections, questions you may have, or a prayer.

_____

_____

_____

_____

_____

_____

_____

_____

_____

_____

_____

_____

CHRIST'S PASSION

DRAWING NEAR

Life, as we all know, is filled with good times and hard times. What have been the three worst days of your life, and why?

_____

_____

_____

Think about what you know of Christ's last days on earth. What does it mean to you personally that Christ suffered so much for you?

_____

_____

_____

THE CONTEXT

Luke recounts in rapid-fire fashion the events of the last days of Christ's Passion Week. On Thursday, the Son of Man and His followers celebrated the Passover. There, in a rented "upper room," Christ instituted a simple meal, called the Lord's Supper, intended to commemorate "the new covenant in My blood." Following Jesus' prediction of His betrayal and Peter's denial, Christ's entourage departed for the Garden of Gethsemane. There, late on Thursday night, Christ agonized in prayer before being arrested.

Then the sad, tragic ending came. The forsaken Son of Man was mocked and savagely beaten, then dragged before the murderous Sanhedrin. Lacking the legal authority to pronounce a death sentence on Jesus, the Jewish council took Him to the Roman governor, Pilate, for a civil trial. Luke 23 ends with the account of Jesus' crucifixion and burial.

KEYS TO THE TEXT

Passover Feast: The Passover was a very special feast day in Israel's religious calendar and was inextricably linked to what took place in the Exodus (Ex. 12–13). It became indelibly entrenched in Israel's tradition and has always marked the day of redemption from Egypt. Passover began with the slaying of the Passover lamb, which had to be a lamb without blemish. Friday of Passover would have begun on Thursday at sunset. According to Josephus, it was customary in his day to slay the lamb at about 3:00 PM. This was the time of day that Christ, the Christian's Passover Lamb, died (1 Cor. 5:7; Luke 23:44–46).

Paradise: It comes from the Greek *paradeisos*, literally, "garden" or "park," and is used to refer to the Garden of Eden. Later, paradise was described as the place of the righteous dead in Sheol (Luke 16:19–31). When Jesus spoke to the thief on the cross, He assured him that he would that day reside with Him in paradise (23:42). This seems to indicate that this word refers to a pleasant place for the righteous among the dead. Revelation 2:7 speaks of paradise as the restitution of an Edenic paradise, an everlasting home for believers (compare Gen. 2 and Rev. 22).

UNLEASHING THE TEXT

Read 22:7–23:56, noting the key words and definitions next to the passage.

the Day of Unleavened Bread (v. 7)—This was the first day of the feast season. The people from Galilee celebrated the Passover on Thursday evening, so the lambs were killed in the afternoon of that day. The disciples and Jesus ate the Passover meal that evening, after sundown.

Go and prepare (v. 8)—This was no small task; the paschal lamb had to be sacrificed and a meal prepared for thirteen people.

a man . . . carrying . . . water (v. 10)—Normally carrying water was woman's work, so a man carrying a pitcher would stand out.

a large, furnished upper room (v. 12)—one of many such rooms for rent in Jerusalem that were maintained for the express purpose of providing pilgrims a place to celebrate feasts

With fervent desire (v. 15)—He wanted to prepare them for what was coming.

Luke 22:7–23:56 (NKJV)

7 Then came the Day of Unleavened Bread, when the Passover must be killed.

8 And He sent Peter and John, saying, "Go and prepare the Passover for us, that we may eat."

9 So they said to Him, "Where do You want us to prepare?"

10 And He said to them, "Behold, when you have entered the city, a man will meet you carrying a pitcher of water; follow him into the house which he enters.

11 Then you shall say to the master of the house, 'The Teacher says to you, "Where is the guest room where I may eat the Passover with My disciples?"'

12 Then he will show you a large, furnished upper room; there make ready."

13 So they went and found it just as He had said to them, and they prepared the Passover.

14 When the hour had come, He sat down, and the twelve apostles with Him.

15 Then He said to them, "With fervent desire I have desired to eat this Passover with you before I suffer;

16 *for I say to you, I will no longer eat of it until it is fulfilled in the kingdom of God."*

17 *Then He took the cup, and gave thanks, and said, "Take this and divide it among yourselves;*

18 *for I say to you, I will not drink of the fruit of the vine until the kingdom of God comes."*

19 *And He took bread, gave thanks and broke it, and gave it to them, saying, "This is My body which is given for you; do this in remembrance of Me."*

20 *Likewise He also took the cup after supper, saying, "This cup is the new covenant in My blood, which is shed for you.*

21 *But behold, the hand of My betrayer is with Me on the table.*

22 *And truly the Son of Man goes as it has been determined, but woe to that man by whom He is betrayed!"*

23 *Then they began to question among themselves, which of them it was who would do this thing.*

24 *Now there was also a dispute among them, as to which of them should be considered the greatest.*

25 *And He said to them, "The kings of the Gentiles exercise lordship over them, and those who exercise authority over them are called 'benefactors.'*

26 *But not so among you; on the contrary, he who is greatest among you, let him be as the younger, and he who governs as he who serves.*

27 *For who is greater, he who sits at the table, or he who serves? Is it not he who sits at the table? Yet I am among you as the One who serves.*

28 *"But you are those who have continued with Me in My trials.*

29 *And I bestow upon you a kingdom, just as My Father bestowed one upon Me,*

30 *that you may eat and drink at My table in My kingdom, and sit on thrones judging the twelve tribes of Israel."*

31 *And the Lord said, "Simon, Simon! Indeed, Satan has asked for you, that he may sift you as wheat.*

Then He took the cup (v. 17)—The Passover seder involved the sharing of four cups of diluted red wine; this cup was the first of the four (the cup of thanksgiving) and was preliminary to the institution of the Lord's Supper.

This is My body (v. 19)—The bread represented His body; such metaphorical language was a typical Hebraism.

remembrance of Me (v. 19)—Passover had looked forward to the sacrifice of Christ; He transformed the seder into an altogether different ceremony, which looks back in remembrance at His atoning death.

the hand of My betrayer is with Me (v. 21)—Luke's words here seem to imply that Judas actually shared in this event; his presence at that table makes his hypocrisy and crime all the more despicable.

but woe (v. 22)—The fact that Judas's betrayal was part of God's plan does not free him from the guilt of a crime he entered into willfully. God's sovereignty is never a legitimate excuse for human guilt.

My trials (v. 28)—Christ's entire life and ministry were filled with temptations (4:1–13), hardships (9:58), sorrows (19:41), and agonies (v. 44)—not to mention the sufferings of the cross which He knew were yet to come.

I bestow upon you a kingdom (v. 29)—Here Christ confirmed the disciples' expectation of an earthly kingdom yet to come, but it would not come in the timing or manner that they hoped.

Satan has asked for you (v. 31)—Though addressed specifically to Peter, this warning embraced the other disciples as well. The pronoun *you* is plural in the Greek text.

that your faith should not fail (v. 32)—Peter himself failed miserably, but his faith was never overthrown (see John 21:18–19).

32 *But I have prayed for you, that your faith should not fail; and when you have returned to Me, strengthen your brethren."*

33 *But he said to Him, "Lord, I am ready to go with You, both to prison and to death."*

34 *Then He said, "I tell you, Peter, the rooster shall not crow this day before you will deny three times that you know Me."*

35 *And He said to them, "When I sent you without money bag, knapsack, and sandals, did you lack anything?" So they said, "Nothing."*

36 *Then He said to them, "But now, he who has a money bag, let him take it, and likewise a knapsack; and he who has no sword, let him sell his garment and buy one.*

37 *For I say to you that this which is written must still be accomplished in Me: 'And He was numbered with the transgressors.' For the things concerning Me have an end."*

two swords (v. 38)—short, daggerlike instruments—more like knives than swords, commonly carried in that culture, because of their practical usefulness

38 *So they said, "Lord, look, here are two swords." And He said to them, "It is enough."*

39 *Coming out, He went to the Mount of Olives, as He was accustomed, and His disciples also followed Him.*

40 *When He came to the place, He said to them, "Pray that you may not enter into temptation."*

about a stone's throw (v. 41)—i.e., within earshot—His prayer was partly for their benefit (see John 11:41–42).

41 *And He was withdrawn from them about a stone's throw, and He knelt down and prayed,*

42 *saying, "Father, if it is Your will, take this cup away from Me; nevertheless not My will, but Yours, be done."*

43 *Then an angel appeared to Him from heaven, strengthening Him.*

44 *And being in agony, He prayed more earnestly. Then His sweat became like great drops of blood falling down to the ground.*

like great drops of blood (v. 44)—This suggests a dangerous condition known as *hematidrosis*, the effusion of blood in one's perspiration, caused by extreme anguish or physical strain; subcutaneous capillaries dilate and burst, mingling blood with sweat.

45 *When He rose up from prayer, and had come to His disciples, He found them sleeping from sorrow.*

46 *Then He said to them, "Why do you sleep? Rise and pray, lest you enter into temptation."*

47 *And while He was still speaking, behold, a multitude; and he who was called Judas, one of the twelve, went before them and drew near to Jesus to kiss Him.*

48 *But Jesus said to him, "Judas, are you betraying the Son of Man with a kiss?"*

49 *When those around Him saw what was going to happen, they said to Him, "Lord, shall we strike with the sword?"*

50 *And one of them struck the servant of the high priest and cut off his right ear.*

51 *But Jesus answered and said, "Permit even this." And He touched his ear and healed him.*

52 *Then Jesus said to the chief priests, captains of the temple, and the elders who had come to Him, "Have you come out, as against a robber, with swords and clubs?*

53 *When I was with you daily in the temple, you did not try to seize Me. But this is your hour, and the power of darkness."*

54 *Having arrested Him, they led Him and brought Him into the high priest's house. But Peter followed at a distance.*

55 *Now when they had kindled a fire in the midst of the courtyard and sat down together, Peter sat among them.*

56 *And a certain servant girl, seeing him as he sat by the fire, looked intently at him and said, "This man was also with Him."*

57 *But he denied Him, saying, "Woman, I do not know Him."*

58 *And after a little while another saw him and said, "You also are of them." But Peter said, "Man, I am not!"*

59 *Then after about an hour had passed, another confidently affirmed, saying, "Surely this fellow also was with Him, for he is a Galilean."*

60 *But Peter said, "Man, I do not know what you are saying!" Immediately, while he was still speaking, the rooster crowed.*

a multitude (v. 47)—heavily armed representatives of the Sanhedrin

touched his ear and healed him (v. 51)—This is the only instance in all of Scripture where Christ healed a fresh wound. It is remarkable that such a dramatic miracle had no effect whatsoever on the hearts of those men.

a certain servant girl (v. 56)—She appears to have been the doorkeeper of Annas's house.

he is a Galilean. (v. 59)—They knew because of his accent (Matt. 26:73).

the Lord turned and looked at Peter (v. 61)—Luke alone records that Jesus made eye contact with Peter; the verb used suggests an intent, fixed look.

As soon as it was day (v. 66)—Criminal trials were not deemed legal if held at night, so the Sanhedrin dutifully waited until daybreak to render the verdict they had already agreed on anyway (see Matt. 26:66; Mark 14:64).

the whole multitude of them (23:1)—The entire Sanhedrin, some seventy men, gathered. At least one member of the council, Joseph of Arimathea, dissented from the decision to condemn Christ (vv. 50–52).

forbidding to pay taxes to Caesar (v. 2)—This was a deliberate lie (see 20:20–25).

61 *And the Lord turned and looked at Peter. Then Peter remembered the word of the Lord, how He had said to him, "Before the rooster crows, you will deny Me three times."*

62 *So Peter went out and wept bitterly.*

63 *Now the men who held Jesus mocked Him and beat Him.*

64 *And having blindfolded Him, they struck Him on the face and asked Him, saying, "Prophesy! Who is the one who struck You?"*

65 *And many other things they blasphemously spoke against Him.*

66 *As soon as it was day, the elders of the people, both chief priests and scribes, came together and led Him into their council, saying,*

67 *"If You are the Christ, tell us." But He said to them, "If I tell you, you will by no means believe.*

68 *And if I also ask you, you will by no means answer Me or let Me go.*

69 *Hereafter the Son of Man will sit on the right hand of the power of God."*

70 *Then they all said, "Are You then the Son of God?" So He said to them, "You rightly say that I am."*

71 *And they said, "What further testimony do we need? For we have heard it ourselves from His own mouth."*

23:1 *Then the whole multitude of them arose and led Him to Pilate.*

2 *And they began to accuse Him, saying, "We found this fellow perverting the nation, and forbidding to pay taxes to Caesar, saying that He Himself is Christ, a King."*

3 *Then Pilate asked Him, saying, "Are You the King of the Jews?" He answered him and said, "It is as you say."*

4 *So Pilate said to the chief priests and the crowd, "I find no fault in this Man."*

5 *But they were the more fierce, saying, "He stirs up the people, teaching throughout all Judea, beginning from Galilee to this place."*

6 *When Pilate heard of Galilee, he asked if the Man were a Galilean.*

7 *And as soon as he knew that He belonged to Herod's jurisdiction, he sent Him to Herod, who was also in Jerusalem at that time.*

8 *Now when Herod saw Jesus, he was exceedingly glad; for he had desired for a long time to see Him, because he had heard many things about Him, and he hoped to see some miracle done by Him.*

9 *Then he questioned Him with many words, but He answered him nothing.*

10 *And the chief priests and scribes stood and vehemently accused Him.*

11 *Then Herod, with his men of war, treated Him with contempt and mocked Him, arrayed Him in a gorgeous robe, and sent Him back to Pilate.*

12 *That very day Pilate and Herod became friends with each other, for previously they had been at enmity with each other.*

13 *Then Pilate, when he had called together the chief priests, the rulers, and the people,*

14 *said to them, "You have brought this Man to me, as one who misleads the people. And indeed, having examined Him in your presence, I have found no fault in this Man concerning those things of which you accuse Him;*

15 *no, neither did Herod, for I sent you back to him; and indeed nothing deserving of death has been done by Him.*

16 *I will therefore chastise Him and release Him"*

17 *(for it was necessary for him to release one to them at the feast).*

18 *And they all cried out at once, saying, "Away with this Man, and release to us Barabbas"—*

19 *who had been thrown into prison for a certain rebellion made in the city, and for murder.*

20 *Pilate, therefore, wishing to release Jesus, again called out to them.*

21 *But they shouted, saying, "Crucify Him, crucify Him!"*

sent Him to Herod (v. 7)—Herod had come to Jerusalem for the feasts, and Pilate seized the opportunity to free himself from a political dilemma by sending Jesus to his rival.

answered him nothing (v. 9)—It is significant that in all Jesus' various interrogations, Herod was the only one to whom He refused to speak; Herod had summarily rejected the truth when he heard it from John the Baptist, so it would have been pointless for Jesus to answer him.

I will . . . chastise Him (v. 16)—Though Pilate found Him innocent of any wrongdoing, he was prepared to scourge Him merely to pacify the Jews.

Crucify Him (v. 21)—Crucifixion was the most painful and disgraceful form of execution the Romans employed.

22 *Then he said to them the third time, "Why, what evil has He done? I have found no reason for death in Him. I will therefore chastise Him and let Him go."*

23 *But they were insistent, demanding with loud voices that He be crucified. And the voices of these men and of the chief priests prevailed.*

24 *So Pilate gave sentence that it should be as they requested.*

25 *And he released to them the one they requested, who for rebellion and murder had been thrown into prison; but he delivered Jesus to their will.*

26 *Now as they led Him away, they laid hold of a certain man, Simon a Cyrenian, who was coming from the country, and on him they laid the cross that he might bear it after Jesus.*

27 *And a great multitude of the people followed Him, and women who also mourned and lamented Him.*

weep for yourselves (v. 28)—Christ's reply to them was a prophetic warning. Only Luke recorded this incident.

28 *But Jesus, turning to them, said, "Daughters of Jerusalem, do not weep for Me, but weep for yourselves and for your children.*

29 *For indeed the days are coming in which they will say, 'Blessed are the barren, wombs that never bore, and breasts which never nursed!'*

30 *Then they will begin 'to say to the mountains, "Fall on us!" and to the hills, "Cover us!"'*

31 *For if they do these things in the green wood, what will be done in the dry?"*

32 *There were also two others, criminals, led with Him to be put to death.*

Calvary (v. 33)—This is the Latin equivalent of *Golgotha*.

33 *And when they had come to the place called Calvary, there they crucified Him, and the criminals, one on the right hand and the other on the left.*

they do not know what they do (v. 34)—They were not aware of the full scope of their wickedness; they were blind to the light of divine truth.

34 *Then Jesus said, "Father, forgive them, for they do not know what they do." And they divided His garments and cast lots.*

35 *And the people stood looking on. But even the rulers with them sneered, saying, "He saved others; let*

Him save Himself if He is the Christ, the chosen of God."

36 The soldiers also mocked Him, coming and offering Him sour wine,

37 and saying, "If You are the King of the Jews, save Yourself."

38 And an inscription also was written over Him in letters of Greek, Latin, and Hebrew: THIS IS THE KING OF THE JEWS.

39 Then one of the criminals who were hanged blasphemed Him, saying, "If You are the Christ, save Yourself and us."

40 But the other, answering, rebuked him, saying, "Do you not even fear God, seeing you are under the same condemnation?

41 And we indeed justly, for we receive the due reward of our deeds; but this Man has done nothing wrong."

42 Then he said to Jesus, "Lord, remember me when You come into Your kingdom."

43 And Jesus said to him, "Assuredly, I say to you, today you will be with Me in Paradise."

44 Now it was about the sixth hour, and there was darkness over all the earth until the ninth hour.

45 Then the sun was darkened, and the veil of the temple was torn in two.

46 And when Jesus had cried out with a loud voice, He said, "Father, 'into Your hands I commit My spirit.'" Having said this, He breathed His last.

47 So when the centurion saw what had happened, he glorified God, saying, "Certainly this was a righteous Man!"

48 And the whole crowd who came together to that sight, seeing what had been done, beat their breasts and returned.

49 But all His acquaintances, and the women who followed Him from Galilee, stood at a distance, watching these things.

50 Now behold, there was a man named Joseph, a council member, a good and just man.

one of the criminals (v. 39)—Matthew 27:44 and Mark 15:32 report that both criminals were mocking Christ along with the crowd; as the hours wore on, however, this criminal's conscience was smitten, and he repented.

Lord, remember me (v. 41)—The penitent thief's prayer reflected his belief that the soul lives on after death, that Christ had a right to rule over a kingdom of the souls of men, and that He would soon enter that kingdom despite His impending death. His request to be remembered was a plea for mercy, which also reveals that the thief understood he had no hope but divine grace and that the dispensing of that grace lay in Jesus' power.

darkness (v. 44)—This could not have been caused by an eclipse, because the Jews used a lunar calendar, and Passover always fell on the full moon, making a solar eclipse out of the question; this was a supernatural darkness.

the women . . . from Galilee (v. 49)—Mary Magdalene; Mary, mother of James (the Less) and Joses; Salome, mother of James and John, and many others. The same women were present at His burial and His resurrection.

143

51 *He had not consented to their decision and deed. He was from Arimathea, a city of the Jews, who himself was also waiting for the kingdom of God.*

52 *This man went to Pilate and asked for the body of Jesus.*

53 *Then he took it down, wrapped it in linen, and laid it in a tomb that was hewn out of the rock, where no one had ever lain before.*

54 *That day was the Preparation, and the Sabbath drew near.*

55 *And the women who had come with Him from Galilee followed after, and they observed the tomb and how His body was laid.*

56 *Then they returned and prepared spices and fragrant oils. And they rested on the Sabbath according to the commandment.*

a tomb . . . hewn out of the rock (v. 53)—Joseph, a wealthy man, undoubtedly had the tomb built for his own family. It had remained unused. Christ's burial there was a wonderful fulfillment of Isaiah 53:9.

1) What light does Exodus 12:1–28 shed on the events of Luke 22:7–18?

_____

_____

_____

2) What surprising event took place immediately following the first Lord's Supper?

_____

_____

_____

3) Describe the scene in Gethsemane (22:39–46). What details stand out?

_____

_____

_____

4) What painful details about Peter's denial does Luke include that the other Gospel writers leave out (see Matt. 26:57–58, 69–75; Mark 14:53–54, 66–72; and John 18:15–18, 25–27)?

_____

_____

_____

5) In Luke's crucifixion account (23:26–46), what does Jesus say and do? List His actions.

_____

_____

_____

Going Deeper

To see the apostle Paul's teaching about the Lord's Supper, read 1 Corinthians 11:20–32.

20 *Therefore when you come together in one place, it is not to eat the Lord's Supper.*

21 *For in eating, each one takes his own supper ahead of others; and one is hungry and another is drunk.*

22 *What! Do you not have houses to eat and drink in? Or do you despise the church of God and shame those who have nothing? What shall I say to you? Shall I praise you in this? I do not praise you.*

23 *For I received from the Lord that which I also delivered to you: that the Lord Jesus on the same night in which He was betrayed took bread;*

24 *and when He had given thanks, He broke it and said, "Take, eat; this is My body which is broken for you; do this in remembrance of Me."*

25 *In the same manner He also took the cup after supper, saying, "This cup is the new covenant in My blood. This do, as often as you drink it, in remembrance of Me."*

26 *For as often as you eat this bread and drink this cup, you proclaim the Lord's death till He comes.*

27 *Therefore whoever eats this bread or drinks this cup of the Lord in an unworthy manner will be guilty of the body and blood of the Lord.*

28 *But let a man examine himself, and so let him eat of the bread and drink of the cup.*

29 *For he who eats and drinks in an unworthy manner eats and drinks judgment to himself, not discerning the Lord's body.*

30 *For this reason many are weak and sick among you, and many sleep.*

31 *For if we would judge ourselves, we would not be judged.*

32 *But when we are judged, we are chastened by the Lord, that we may not be condemned with the world.*

Exploring the Meaning

6) What issues concerned the apostle Paul about the Corinthian church's practice of observing the Lord's Supper?

_____

_____

_____

_____

7) What made Christ's experience in Gethsemane so excruciating?

_____

_____

_____

8) What evidences of Christ's deity and lordship do you see in these chapters?

_____

_____

_____

_____

Truth for Today

Jesus Christ evokes many images in the minds of people. Some picture Him as a baby in a manger—the Christ of Christmas. Others picture Him as a child, perhaps living in the home of a carpenter or confounding the religious leaders of Jerusalem. Many picture Him as a compassionate and powerful healer who restored the sick and raised the dead. Still others picture a bold and fiery preacher speaking the Word of God to great crowds. And there are those who see Him as the consummate man—a model of goodness, kindness, sympathy, concern, care, tenderness, forgiveness, wisdom, and understanding.

Yet the one image of Christ that surpasses all the rest is Jesus Christ on the cross. To know Christ crucified is to know Him as the author and finisher of your faith—the truest picture of His Person and work. Christ's suffering on the cross is the focal point of the Christian faith. That's where His deity, humanity, work, and suffering are most clearly seen.

REFLECTING ON THE TEXT

9) Reflect on Christ's dying for you on the cross. Considering Luke's account, what touches you most, moves you, motivates you to want to live for Him today?

_____

_____

_____

_____

_____

10) What will you take from this study into your next celebration of the Lord's Supper?

_____

_____

_____

_____

11) Luke 22:7–23:56 is a gritty, hard-to-stomach passage. But what are the bright spots here? Are there any actions that are noteworthy and worth emulating?

_____

_____

_____

_____

PERSONAL RESPONSE

Write out additional reflections, questions you may have, or a prayer.

~ 12 ~
CHRIST IS RISEN!

Luke 24:1–53

DRAWING NEAR

What is the best Easter celebration/worship service you have experienced?
What was special about it?

_____

_____

_____

What surprises you about Jesus' resurrection? What, if any, questions do
you still have about it?

_____

_____

_____

THE CONTEXT

We've seen Jesus' miraculous birth, amazing life and teachings, and sacrificial
death. But the story is not over. The final chapter of Luke's gospel documents
Christ's victory over the grave! In this closing section, we also hear Jesus'
commission to His followers to take the good news to the ends of the earth.
There are also several ideas that are echoed in the opening of the book of Acts
(also written by Luke), including Christ's suffering and resurrection, the message
of repentance and remission of sins, and the disciples sent as His witnesses.

KEYS TO THE TEXT

Resurrection: A central doctrine of the Christian faith. Paul reminded the
Corinthian Christians that they already believed in Christ's resurrection, else they
would not have been Christians. Because Christ was raised, resurrection from the
dead obviously is possible; and, on the other hand, unless men in general can be
resurrected, Christ could not have been raised. The two resurrections stand or
fall together; there could not be one without the other. Furthermore, if there is no
resurrection, the gospel is meaningless and worthless. Through Adam we have
inherited our natural bodies; through Christ we will inherit spiritual bodies in the
resurrection. Christ's resurrection was the prototype of all subsequent resurrection.

149

Preach: Jesus said that the good news of salvation should be preached to all nations. From the Greek word *kerusso*, it means "to proclaim" or "to publish"; that is, to publicly make a message known. Preaching is the proclamation of certainties, not the suggestion of possibilities. The faithful preacher and teacher will proclaim God's certain truth, with God's delegated authority, and under God's divine commission.

UNLEASHING THE TEXT

Read Luke 24:1–53, noting the key words and definitions next to the passage.

Luke 24:1–53 (NKJV)

bringing the spices (v. 1)—The women were not expecting to find Jesus risen from the dead; their only plan was to finish anointing His body for burial.

the stone rolled away (v. 2)—Matthew 28:2–4 records that an earthquake occurred and an angel rolled the stone away; the Roman guards fainted with fear.

two men (v. 4)—These were angels.

1 Now on the first day of the week, very early in the morning, they, and certain other women with them, came to the tomb bringing the spices which they had prepared.

2 But they found the stone rolled away from the tomb.

3 Then they went in and did not find the body of the Lord Jesus.

4 And it happened, as they were greatly perplexed about this, that behold, two men stood by them in shining garments.

5 Then, as they were afraid and bowed their faces to the earth, they said to them, "Why do you seek the living among the dead?

6 He is not here, but is risen! Remember how He spoke to you when He was still in Galilee,

7 saying, 'The Son of Man must be delivered into the hands of sinful men, and be crucified, and the third day rise again.'"

8 And they remembered His words.

9 Then they returned from the tomb and told all these things to the eleven and to all the rest.

Mary Magdalene (v. 10)—She was the first to see Jesus alive.

10 It was Mary Magdalene, Joanna, Mary the mother of James, and the other women with them, who told these things to the apostles.

idle tales (v. 11)—i.e., nonsense

11 And their words seemed to them like idle tales, and they did not believe them.

12 But Peter arose and ran to the tomb; and stooping down, he saw the linen cloths lying by themselves;

and he departed, marveling to himself at what had happened.

13 *Now behold, two of them were traveling that same day to a village called Emmaus, which was seven miles from Jerusalem.*

14 *And they talked together of all these things which had happened.*

15 *So it was, while they conversed and reasoned, that Jesus Himself drew near and went with them.*

16 *But their eyes were restrained, so that they did not know Him.*

17 *And He said to them, "What kind of conversation is this that you have with one another as you walk and are sad?"*

18 *Then the one whose name was Cleopas answered and said to Him, "Are You the only stranger in Jerusalem, and have You not known the things which happened there in these days?"*

19 *And He said to them, "What things?" So they said to Him, "The things concerning Jesus of Nazareth, who was a Prophet mighty in deed and word before God and all the people,*

20 *and how the chief priests and our rulers delivered Him to be condemned to death, and crucified Him.*

21 *But we were hoping that it was He who was going to redeem Israel. Indeed, besides all this, today is the third day since these things happened.*

22 *Yes, and certain women of our company, who arrived at the tomb early, astonished us.*

23 *When they did not find His body, they came saying that they had also seen a vision of angels who said He was alive.*

24 *And certain of those who were with us went to the tomb and found it just as the women had said; but Him they did not see."*

25 *Then He said to them, "O foolish ones, and slow of heart to believe in all that the prophets have spoken!*

26 *Ought not the Christ to have suffered these things and to enter into His glory?"*

two of them (v. 13)—These evidently were not any of the eleven disciples; according to verse 18, one was named Cleopas.

their eyes were restrained (v. 16)—They were kept by God from recognizing Him.

But we were hoping (v. 21)—They had been looking for an immediate earthly kingdom; with Jesus crucified, they were probably struggling with doubt about whether He was the Messiah who would reign.

in all the Scriptures (v. 27)—In the inscrutable wisdom of divine providence, the substance of Christ's exposition of the Old Testament messianic prophecies was not recorded; but the gist of what He expounded would have undoubtedly included an explanation of the Old Testament sacrificial system, which was full of types and symbols that spoke of His sufferings and death. He also would have pointed them to the major prophetic passages about Messiah.

their eyes were opened (v. 31)—They had been sovereignly kept from recognizing Him until this point (see v. 16). His resurrection body was glorified and altered from its previous appearance (see John's description in Revelation 1:13–16), and this surely explains why even Mary did not recognize Him at first (see John 20:14–16). But in this case, God actively intervened to keep them from recognizing Him until it was time for Him to depart.

Jesus Himself stood in the midst of them (v. 36)—The doors were closed and locked.

Behold My hands and My feet (v. 39)—He was showing them the nail wounds to prove it was really Him.

27 *And beginning at Moses and all the Prophets, He expounded to them in all the Scriptures the things concerning Himself.*

28 *Then they drew near to the village where they were going, and He indicated that He would have gone farther.*

29 *But they constrained Him, saying, "Abide with us, for it is toward evening, and the day is far spent." And He went in to stay with them.*

30 *Now it came to pass, as He sat at the table with them, that He took bread, blessed and broke it, and gave it to them.*

31 *Then their eyes were opened and they knew Him; and He vanished from their sight.*

32 *And they said to one another, "Did not our heart burn within us while He talked with us on the road, and while He opened the Scriptures to us?"*

33 *So they rose up that very hour and returned to Jerusalem, and found the eleven and those who were with them gathered together,*

34 *saying, "The Lord is risen indeed, and has appeared to Simon!"*

35 *And they told about the things that had happened on the road, and how He was known to them in the breaking of bread.*

36 *Now as they said these things, Jesus Himself stood in the midst of them, and said to them, "Peace to you."*

37 *But they were terrified and frightened, and supposed they had seen a spirit.*

38 *And He said to them, "Why are you troubled? And why do doubts arise in your hearts?*

39 *Behold My hands and My feet, that it is I Myself. Handle Me and see, for a spirit does not have flesh and bones as you see I have."*

40 *When He had said this, He showed them His hands and His feet.*

41 *But while they still did not believe for joy, and marveled, He said to them, "Have you any food here?"*

42 *So they gave Him a piece of a broiled fish and some honeycomb.*

⁴³ *And He took it and ate in their presence.*

⁴⁴ *Then He said to them, "These are the words which I spoke to you while I was still with you, that all things must be fulfilled which were written in the Law of Moses and the Prophets and the Psalms concerning Me."*

⁴⁵ *And He opened their understanding, that they might comprehend the Scriptures.*

⁴⁶ *Then He said to them, "Thus it is written, and thus it was necessary for the Christ to suffer and to rise from the dead the third day,*

⁴⁷ *and that repentance and remission of sins should be preached in His name to all nations, beginning at Jerusalem.*

⁴⁸ *And you are witnesses of these things.*

⁴⁹ *Behold, I send the Promise of My Father upon you; but tarry in the city of Jerusalem until you are endued with power from on high."*

⁵⁰ *And He led them out as far as Bethany, and He lifted up His hands and blessed them.*

⁵¹ *Now it came to pass, while He blessed them, that He was parted from them and carried up into heaven.*

⁵² *And they worshiped Him, and returned to Jerusalem with great joy,*

⁵³ *and were continually in the temple praising and blessing God. Amen.*

opened their understanding (v. 45)—This seems to convey a supernatural opening of their minds to receive the truths He unfolded. Whereas their understanding was once dull (9:45), they finally saw clearly.

carried up into heaven (v. 51)—Before, when the resurrected Christ left them, He simply vanished (v. 31); this time they saw Him ascend.

in the temple (v. 53)—This became the first meeting-place of the church (Acts 2:46; 5:21, 42).

1) Who were the initial visitors to Christ's tomb? (Note: See the other Gospels for more details.)

_____

_____

2) What was the scene at the tomb? What events unfolded upon their arrival?

_____

_____

3) Summarize Luke's record of the incident on the road to Emmaus (vv. 13–32).

_____

_____

4) What evidences does Luke give in this chapter that Christ came back from the grave with a physical body and not merely as a spirit?

_____

_____

_____

5) What instructions did Jesus leave for His disciples before returning to heaven?

_____

_____

_____

GOING DEEPER

The apostle Paul taught about the importance of the resurrection. Read 1 Corinthians 15:3–22.

3 *For I delivered to you first of all that which I also received: that Christ died for our sins according to the Scriptures,*

4 *and that He was buried, and that He rose again the third day according to the Scriptures,*

5 *and that He was seen by Cephas, then by the twelve.*

6 *After that He was seen by over five hundred brethren at once, of whom the greater part remain to the present, but some have fallen asleep.*

7 *After that He was seen by James, then by all the apostles.*

8 *Then last of all He was seen by me also, as by one born out of due time.*

9 *For I am the least of the apostles, who am not worthy to be called an apostle, because I persecuted the church of God.*

10 *But by the grace of God I am what I am, and His grace toward me was not in vain; but I labored more abundantly than they all, yet not I, but the grace of God which was with me.*

11 *Therefore, whether it was I or they, so we preach and so you believed.*

12 *Now if Christ is preached that He has been raised from the dead, how do some among you say that there is no resurrection of the dead?*

13 *But if there is no resurrection of the dead, then Christ is not risen.*

14 *And if Christ is not risen, then our preaching is empty and your faith is also empty.*

15 *Yes, and we are found false witnesses of God, because we have testified of*

God that He raised up Christ, whom He did not raise up—if in fact the dead do not rise.

16 *For if the dead do not rise, then Christ is not risen.*

17 *And if Christ is not risen, your faith is futile; you are still in your sins!*

18 *Then also those who have fallen asleep in Christ have perished.*

19 *If in this life only we have hope in Christ, we are of all men the most pitiable.*

20 *But now Christ is risen from the dead, and has become the firstfruits of those who have fallen asleep.*

21 *For since by man came death, by Man also came the resurrection of the dead.*

22 *For as in Adam all die, even so in Christ all shall be made alive.*

EXPLORING THE MEANING

6) According to Paul, why is the bodily resurrection of Christ so central to the Christian faith?

_____

_____

7) What is significant about Luke's statement in 24:52 that "they worshiped Him"?

_____

_____

8) Christ's resurrection body, though real and tangible, nonetheless was altered in a mysterious way. Luke 24:31 says that Christ vanished from their sight. His body could pass through solid objects (John 20:19, 26). What conclusions can you draw about Jesus' glorified body?

_____

_____

9) To what power is Christ referring when He commands His disciples to wait in the city until they have been given the power promised from above?

_____

_____

TRUTH FOR TODAY

The resurrection of Jesus Christ is the single greatest event in the history of the world. It is so foundational to Christianity that no one who denies it can be a true Christian. Without resurrection there is no Christian faith, no salvation, and no hope. The foundation of all our hope is expressed in Jesus' own words: "I am the resurrection and the life. He who believes in Me, though he may die, he shall live" (John 11:25 NKJV).

REFLECTING ON THE TEXT

10) The Lord Jesus gave His followers the mission of taking the gospel to the ends of the earth. What are you doing to see this goal fulfilled? What percentage of your prayers, giving, conversation, time, and energy is devoted to proclaiming the good news of a risen Savior?

_____

_____

11) We have come to the end of our study of Luke's Gospel. Take a few moments to think back over these twelve lessons.

⌁ What new insights have you gained about the Person of Christ? How has your understanding of Him changed?

⌁ What event or teaching has had the greatest impact on you?

⌁ How has your love for Christ deepened?

⌁ In what new and specific ways are you motivated to live for Him?

_____

_____

_____

PERSONAL RESPONSE

Write out additional reflections, questions you may have, or a prayer.

_____

_____

_____